Urban Anthropology

Urban Anthropology
Cities in Their Cultural Settings

RICHARD G. FOX
Duke University

Prentice-Hall, Inc., Englewood Cliffs, New Jersey 07632

Library of Congress Cataloging in Publication Data

FOX, RICHARD GABRIEL, (date)
  Urban anthropology.

  Bibliography: p.
  Includes index.
  1. Urban anthropology. 2. Cities and towns.
I. Title.
GN395.F69   301.36'3   76-41214
ISBN 0-13-939462-1

© 1977 by Prentice-Hall, Inc., Englewood Cliffs, New Jersey 07632

PRENTICE-HALL SERIES IN ANTHROPOLOGY
David M. Schneider, Series Editor

Printed in the United States of America

10 9 8 7 6 5 4 3 2 1

Prentice-Hall International, Inc., *London*
Prentice-Hall of Australia Pty. Limited, *Sydney*
Prentice-Hall of Canada, Ltd., *Toronto*
Prentice-Hall of India Private Limited, *New Delhi*
Prentice-Hall of Japan, Inc., *Tokyo*
Prentice-Hall of Southeast Asia Pte. Ltd., *Singapore*
Whitehall Book Limited, Wellington, *New Zealand*

To My Favorite Sociologist

Contents

Preface

Some scholars claim anthropology is dead—outmoded in a nuclear world without spears, hoes, tumplines, outriggers, and the primitives who used them. The last decades have witnessed often exaggerated reports of other deaths—the end of ideology, of God, of ethnicity, of the family. The genesis of this book lay in my own fear that anthropology was indeed dead; its present format is a personal and, one hopes, scholarly affirmation that the reports of anthropology's demise have in fact been greatly exaggerated. If anthropology could say new things about cities, if anthropologists could carry forth effective research in urban locales, I reasoned, then surely the discipline was alive and well and living in the complex present rather than expiring with the primitive past. This quest led me to study urban institutions and their cultural settings in many different societies and time periods, and in ways rather different from much current urban anthropology. Yet in comparing the urbanism of contemporary Swaziland with that of Charlemagne, or of a north Indian town with seventeenth-century Paris, I only follow a long tradition of comparative research instituted by Morgan, Maine, Durkheim, and Mauss that sought to illuminate (often quite incorrectly) the present from the past. The presentiments of anthropology's demise have been with us, I believe, ever since many anthropologists rebuked this comparative approach as the discipline became professionalized several generations ago. Using this viewpoint for the study of cities continues to make anthropology vital for me. I hope it will appear in the same fashion to the readers of this volume.

I owe a great deal to the Institute for Advanced Study at Princeton for permitting me the time to develop my fears about anthropology's future and the solitude to resolve these fears within the context of urban anthropology. Clifford Geertz, in his writings and as a colleague at the Institute, also helped with this task. My greatest debt is to the students in my introductory and urban anthropology classes who sometimes corrected and argued, often supported, and generally suffered my preliminary formulations on cities in their cultural settings. I thank especially Ken Dane and Louis Cimino. David Schneider and Ed Stanford also encouraged this work in its initial stages, while Alice Harvey and the staff at Prentice-Hall greatly improved its final form.

Finally, I wish to thank the National Institute of Mental Health, which provided the funding for my fieldwork in Newport and Charleston under grant number 5RO1–MH–18336.

RICHARD G. FOX
Durham, North Carolina

Urban Anthropology

1

Anthropology and the City

Because anthropological interest in cities is recent and still developing, no consensus presently exists as to what questions urban anthropologists should ask and what problems urban anthropology is capable of solving.[1] The trickle of urban anthropological studies that began shortly before World War II has now in the wake of the colonial period and the American civil rights movement become a tide of research. Nevertheless, the richness of urban research possibilities and the challenge of new avenues in anthropology have produced both a variety of approaches in urban anthropology and an emphasis on collection of field data rather than theoretical analysis. The most significant common understandings among urban anthropologists are that cities are important research locales and that anthropology is able to make important methodological and theoretical contributions to the study of urban places. Beyond this agreement lie several different urban anthropologies, each accentuating certain characteristic features of anthropology

---

[1]Cf. Jack R. Rollwagen, "Introduction," *Urban Anthropology*, IV, 1 (Spring, 1975), p. 002: "The most noticeable aspect of urban anthropology at this point in time is that very little generalization is being done at any level. The very name 'urban anthropology' is under attack. Some claim that there is no such thing as 'urban anthropology.' Others claim that even if there were, it would not be important. For others, the argument is that urban anthropology is only anthropology done in urban places. For yet others, urban anthropology is just sociology done by individuals who lack the competence to conduct such investigations."

1

and denying others, analyzing certain kinds of cities and ignoring others. Each of these perspectives assumes the label "urban anthropology," as we will see in the following sections that trace these perspectives' development and approach. However, the conceptions of the city and the definitions of the anthropologist's role in the urban area differ markedly from one perspective to another.

To understand the varieties of urban anthropology, we must briefly trace anthropology's development as a discipline. We must see what viewpoints and methods characterize its approach to the study of human behavior, and how the several urban anthropologies have selected different aspects of the common anthropological tradition to emphasize. Anthropology's unique approach to the definition and study of urban phenomena will also emerge from this brief review.

HOLISM, PARTICIPANT OBSERVATION, AND CROSS-CULTURAL COMPARISON

Why is anthropology so often identified in popular sentiment as the study of primitive peoples? Why have anthropologists only very recently undertaken the study of urban people and urban locales? The answer to these questions lies in the history of anthropology and its emergence as a scholarly discipline.

An ever-widening view of man and his societies characterizes the development of anthropology as a professional scholarly discipline from the early twentieth century. At the outset, anthropologists studied primitive peoples in far-off places. In the last thirty years, peasant communities in the underdeveloped nations of the world have increasingly come under the scrutiny of anthropology. Most recently, urban areas and their populations have entered the inventory of human groups that anthropologists study. Although research is widely dispersed geographically, although the human conditions under study range from the most rudimentary band to the most complex industrial urban locale, and although very divergent theoretical positions obtain in the field, anthropology as a discipline has a common core of understandings about human society and culture. The nature of anthropology as a scholarly discipline, its methods of data collection, theoretical constructs, and style of proof ultimately derive from its professional development in the study of the primitive world. These fundamental characteristics of the discipline condition anthropology's approach to the study of urban areas and its ultimate contribution to conceptions of the city. But these same characteristics also explain the delay and difficulty in weaving urban research into anthropology's design.

Anthropologists in the early twentieth century came to see the prime determinants of different human ways of life as the pattern of social behavior and the rules that governed that behavior within any given society—quite apart from both individual psychological makeup and racial stock. Since these rules and patterns of social intercourse determine the form or configuration of an entire society and make it unique, the anthropologist can best understand each society by studying it as a whole. This "holistic" approach to other societies lies behind two fundamental and complementary concepts accepted by many anthropologists: that any given society forms an integrated social system, and that its culture can be analyzed apart from the many individual actors who function in it.

Approaching a society as an integrated social system assumes that societies are not merely random and disorganized collections of people, but that they have ongoing patterns of relationship and behavior that build up between members over the course of long-standing interaction. Such behavior patterns, which generally pass down over many generations (although sometimes highly modified), form the social organization or social structure of a society. Social organization is most easily perceived in the institutions of a society; for example, the behavioral patterns associated with the family, the interactional aspects of politics, and the methods of socially organizing the religious experience in churches or other ritual centers. Such institutions differ in each human society. When generalized by the anthropologist into a view of social organization in any specific society, these institutions indicate how the Nuer differ from the Bemba or how Hindu civilization differs from American society. Since the anthropologist treats a society as an organized social system, its institutions are seen as interlinked and functionally interdependent (although this functional integration has often been exaggerated). The organization of religious institutions affects the organization of the family; change in the political institutions of the society may alter or influence the rest of the social order.

What lie behind the interrelated institutions of a society and its resulting social organization are rules—much as the behavior on a baseball field is patterned by a plan of the game that all players follow to the best of their abilities. Some of these rules emerge from the technological level of the society. Where boats do not exist, the economic institutions of a society cannot depend on deep-sea fishing. Nor can societies lacking alcoholic beverages have social institutions such as bars. Other rules grow out of the ideological pattern of the society: Hindus should be vegetarian; Kwakiutls should burn property and give lavish feasts; Mus-

lims must seclude their women and not drink wine. The sum of these
rules —whether technologically or ideologically derived—determines an
individual's behavior as a member of a particular society and helps
create a uniformity of belief and action that makes Hindus act more like
other Hindus than like Americans, Bushmen, or Kwakiutls. Anthropologists refer to the sum of such rules as the "culture" of a specific society
and use this concept to explain why societies are organized social systems
and why they function as interrelated wholes.[2]

Anthropologists approach cultures as if they stood apart from the
many individuals who are their constituents in a biological sense. We set
aside the thousands of individuals and the millions of bits of individual
behavior that make up the institutions of any society. Instead, the anthropologist, for heuristic purposes, conceives a culture as systemic; he
investigates the cultural rules that govern the society's operation as
distinct from individuals' actions in the social system.

A discipline that emphasizes how each society has a distinctive
culture and social organization may easily fall into mere description of
the range of human social variation found throughout the world. Cross-
cultural comparison of social organization has been the method by which
anthropology has sought general insight into human development and
capabilities. Nineteenth-century scholars lifted social institutions piece-
meal out of diverse cultures in order to erect monumental (and errone-
ous) schemes of the evolution of the family, religion, or private property.
In their contemporary cross-cultural comparisons, however, anthropologists are extremely wary of taking any single institution out of
the context of its society and culture and comparing it with another
society's institution similarly forcibly excised from its surrounding culture pattern. For comparisons to be meaningful, they must be based on a
holistic contrasting of societies and cultural patterns.

The holistic approach to social organization, culture, and cross-cultural comparison—an approach that originates in the study of primitive
peoples—is what makes anthropology a distinctive professional discipline. Two goals of urban anthropology, the branch of the discipline
that studies cities, are to maintain this holistic view of urban places and to
analyze them in relation to the societies and cultures in which they occur.
Such programmatic goals are easier to set than to carry forward. As we
will see, several very different interpretations of their scholarly role in

---

[2]American anthropologists have offered many definitions of culture, and disagree-
ment exists as to its exact definition in some cases. See A.L. Kroeber and Clyde Kluckhohn,
Culture: A Critical Review of Concepts and Definitions (Cambridge, Massachusetts: The
Museum, 1952) for a list of 161 definitions and Charles A. Valentine, *Culture and Poverty:
Critique and Counter-Proposals* (Chicago: University of Chicago Press, 1968), pp. 1-5, for a
discussion of the culture concept.

the city have been advocated by anthropologists. Some go so far as to claim that research done in cities cannot by definition be anthropology. Why this disagreement or even denial of anthropology's value to city studies? Why does the city enter so recently and still so tentatively into a discipline called the science of mankind?

Part of the hesitancy comes from the difficulties of pursuing a holistic and cross-cultural viewpoint in such a complex phenomenon as urbanism. Thousands of cities containing millions of people in hundreds of cultures presently exist. If the cities of past cultures are included, this figure would be multiplied many times. The sheer numbers involved in urban life, the complexity of urban social institutions, and the diversity of urban life-ways challenge the anthropologist's holistic cultural approach and his cross-cultural generalizations, successful though they may be or may have been in primitive societies. The result is a diversity of viewpoints in urban anthropology, even to the extent that some urban anthropologists do not follow a holistic approach; they set aside cross-cultural comparison in urban research. Instead, they emphasize other characteristics of anthropology that emerged from its professional genesis in the study of primitive societies—characteristics to which we now turn.

Primitive societies were generally small and self-contained. The methodology that anthropology developed to study them in the early twentieth century emphasized lengthy *in situ* contact by the researcher, who was both participant and observer. Rather than sampling surveys or compiling aggregate data, rather than mapping regions or quantifying electoral behavior, anthropologists lived among and often as members of the primitive societies they studied. The benefit from this intensive, small-scale research was that the anthropologist followed the actual flow of social life; the amity and enmity of individuals, families, and kin groups; the ceremonial round, the subsistence pattern. He not only asked what people believed and how they acted; he also saw these beliefs affirmed or contradicted in the everyday lives and ceremonies of the people he lived with—in their feasts, marriages, initiations, and warfare. No other discipline commits its adherents to the same degree of intensive interaction. Consequently few disciplines other than anthropology can create a similar total picture, at once intimate and realistic, of social life in other societies.

Even though it remains an essential characteristic of anthropology, this small-scale and highly personal research technique has undergone modifications as anthropologists have moved from primitive societies to peasant communities and thence to urban locales. Such participant-observer techniques often led anthropologists to ignore the outside force impinging on their primitive peoples and to treat these peoples as isolates from both surrounding societies and world society. When anthropologists moved to the study of India, Latin America, or China, they continued the pattern of small-scale research by locating themselves in the rural peasant communities that form one part of these complex societies. Treating peasant communities as isolates became increasingly inappropriate as anthropologists learned of their economic, political, and ideological links to the nation and region. By concentrating on the social life of a single village, anthropologists had grave difficulties in understanding or even perceiving the social organization and cultural rules of the entire society. Peasant studies in recent years have moved away from viewing rural communities as isolates and towards perceiving their interrelations with the large society of which they are a part.[3] In spite of this modification, anthropologists have generally maintained their small-scale approach and intensive participant-observer techniques. They have, however, gradually become more sensitive to the links between their local communities and the surrounding society.

Small-scale participant observation techniques offer similar attractions and benefits to urban anthropology but also carry the same limitations. In order to continue the intensive research methods derived from studies of primitive societies, urban anthropologists often select highly visible but socially segregated urban populations living in slums, ghettos, or shanty towns. Because they are commonly impoverished and often racially or economically distinct from the urban mainstream, the researcher treats these segregated groups as if they corresponded to the small-scale and self-contained (primitive) society of an earlier anthropology. Such urban populations are sometimes even said to have a culture different from the urban mainstream. By probing deeply into the life-ways of these outcast and disfranchised urban dwellers, the anthropologist is able to maintain his customary small-scale research methods. However, he also runs the risk (as did his colleagues who initiated peasant studies) of saying little about the city as a whole or the cross-cultural validity of his findings.

In the next section of this chapter, we will more specifically differentiate the urban anthropology that follows the holistic tradition from the urban anthropology that accentuates participant observation techniques. At this point, it is important to see how both these perspectives are outgrowths of anthropology's development, and how in the original anthropological study of primitive societies, the holistic ap-

---

[3]Cf. Eric R. Wolf, *Peasants* (Englewood Cliffs, New Jersey: Prentice-Hall, Inc., 1966) and G. William Skinner, "Chinese Peasants and the Closed Community: An Open and Shut Case," *Comparative Studies in Society and History*, XIII (1971), pp. 272-73.

proach neatly dovetailed with such small-scale, intensive research techniques. Unfortunately, these two anthropological traditions do not fit together nearly so neatly in researching the complexities of urban social institutions and life-ways. Indeed they are sometimes even contradictory, given certain questions the anthropologist may wish to resolve in his urban research. Depending on whether he emphasizes the holistic tradition or the participant-observer method, the urban anthropologist will adopt very different goals in the city, will select different social phenomena for study, and will set his findings in a different scholarly context.

Another distinction within urban anthropology arises from the time dimension adopted in city studies. Most primitive societies were non-literate and therefore lacked a written history (as distinct from oral traditions). Although some of the pioneer nineteenth-century anthropologists traced the origins of institutions and the historical diffusion of material culture, their reconstructions were often fanciful and their data insufficient. Such improper methods led anthropology early in its professional development to abandon this "spurious" history and to emphasize a synchronic approach. A synchronic viewpoint means that the time period during which the anthropologist actually saw a society sets the temporal limits for his analysis of it. The synchronic framework applied to primitive societies by anthropologists was thus a technique to do away with conjectural history and to perceive a society better as a (contemporary) social system.

Although it may have been defensible in studies of primitive societies, researching the city in a synchronic fashion greatly restricts the anthropologist's comprehension of how contemporary cities have developed and removes from his analysis types of cities that may no longer exist. However, some anthropologists continue this synchronic analysis in their urban research because they deal with problems (such as urbanization in third-world countries) that are present-day. Such contemporary problems as these presumably are not amenable to a diachronic perspective, which deals with societies as they change over time. Like participant observation techniques, synchronic analysis combined easily with a holistic perspective in the anthropology of primitive societies. They do not combine easily in urban research, and anthropologists who follow the holistic tradition and those who carry forward the synchronic one often go very separate ways in the city.

Another legacy of the discipline's early concern with the primitive world is a pursuit of the exotic, the strange, the arcane, and the outré in human behavior. Anthropologists have often viewed themselves as specialists in the great variety of social patterns found within the human

species. As an extension, they commonly accentuate their scholarly status as possessors of the odd lore of distant and unknown societies. This
pursuit of the exotic in human societies and global culture is no discredit
to anthropology, for it has given the discipline a breadth of involvement
with humanity that other social sciences rarely achieve. It has provided
information on life-ways that were either bypassed or threatened with
extinction by the colonial or industrial juggernaut of Western civilization. It brought under scrutiny a wide variety of societal and cultural
types. Anthropology has thus greatly furthered cross-cultural analysis
and corrected the ethnocentrisms inherent in many social sciences that
implicitly took Western society as a model.

Pursuit of the romantic lies behind the concentration on ghetto
people or recent migrants to the city found in much urban anthropology
today. In the metropolises of industrial American society or in the native
locations of colonial Africa the anthropologist recreates in an urban
context his traditional role of studying people "for whom no other
discipline cares."[4] But urban anthropology lives in and must cope with a
world of modernization and urbanization, of mass culture and high-rise
existence, of wars for national liberation, and of post-colonialism. Urban
anthropologists who reincarnate primitive romanticism in the context of
the contemporary urban world usually ignore mainstream social classes
and communities and their power and policy in the city (which often
represent the controlling fates of the poor and outcast among whom
these urban anthropologists specialize). Such an approach risks maintaining a traditional characteristic of anthropology at the expense of our
ability to cope with urban research. Perhaps more than anything else,
anthropology's pursuit of the romantic and foreign is why it abjured
cities until very recently and why the utility or viability of urban research
remains moot for many anthropologists even now.

Anthropology's unique viewpoint in the social sciences emerges
from the discipline's involvement with the primitive world. Holism,
cross-cultural comparison, small-scale participant observation, and a
synchronic approach all neatly combined in early studies. They formed
the romantic quest for human behavior at its antipodes that came to be
anthropology. Unfortunately these various elements do not easily remain in combination when anthropologists study complex societies and
cities. By selecting either holism or participant observation or a synchronic approach, various urban anthropologists define their research

    [4]John Gulick, "Urban Anthropology: Its Present and Future," in *Readings in An-
thropology*, 2nd ed., Morton H. Fried, ed. (New York: Thomas Y. Crowell Company, 1968),
pp. 560-61.

goals differently, go to different kinds of cities, and study different sorts of dwellers within them. The next section discusses three varieties of urban anthropology, or more properly, three distinct perspectives about what urban studies should mean in anthropology.

URBANISM, POVERTY, AND URBANIZATION

To talk of a single urban anthropology at present is to give a false impression of conceptual agreement and clarity. Several different and sometimes conflicting urban anthropologies exist, each accentuating certain characteristics of anthropology (as discussed previously) and denying others. This diversity reflects in part the newness of urban anthropology and its unformed state. In part these differences reflect separate scholarly traditions within anthropology, as for instance between American cultural anthropology and British social anthropology. This section reviews the three major viewpoints in urban anthropology—the anthropology of urbanism, the anthropology of poverty, and the anthropology of urbanization—and discusses their strengths and limitations and their specialization in certain kinds of cities.

The Anthropology of Urbanism

The *anthropology of urbanism* represents the first urban anthropology, one which emphasized anthropology's holistic approach and cross-cultural perspective. Robert Redfield's *The Folk Culture of Yucatan* (1941)[5] indicated that the city could be a proper locale for anthropological research and defined the folk-urban continuum as a holistic and cross-cultural model for its investigation. Redfield's notion was that as folk communities evolved into urban societies, they changed from small, self-contained, isolated, highly personalized, religious, and traditional social locales into large, heterogeneous, impersonal, secular, and innovative social milieus.[6] Subsequent scholarship by Gideon Sjoberg and Oscar Lewis has sharply questioned Redfield's implicit acceptance of

[5]Robert Redfield, *The Folk Culture of Yucatan* (Chicago: The University of Chicago Press, 1941).
[6]Robert Redfield, "The Folk Society," *The American Journal of Sociology*, LII, 4 (1947), pp. 306-308.

industrial cities as a universal urban model.[7] Thus, Sjoberg distinguishes between "preindustrial" and "industrial" cities, asserting that the former do not share the characteristics of impersonality, secularism, and great size assumed in the folk-urban hypothesis. In a different vein, Oscar Lewis found that migrants to Mexico City did not suffer the family breakdown by which Redfield typified urban existence.

Although the specific image of urbanism utilized in the folk-urban continuum was too heavily pinned to Western industrial cities, as Redfield himself shortly realized, his approach to the city as an emergent level of cultural evolution or as a highly evolved social institution defined the initial viewpoint for anthropologists in the city. Other scholars, like Milton Singer, Horace Miner, Conrad Arensberg, John Gulick, and Anthony Leeds,[8] continue to investigate those qualities of urban life and social institutions that differentiate it from primitive societies and peasant communities. Their scholarly concern for the special qualities of urbanism leads these urban anthropologists to a holistic view of how cities are linked to the societies in which they occur. In this approach, cities appear as realms of social life inextricably bound—as either receptor or generator—to the institutions and values of the society in which they are set. They investigate the cultural roles played by cities within their societies, and they cross-culturally analyze cities with distinctive physical forms and internal social organization.

For example, in correcting the initial folk-urban formulation, Redfield and Singer delineated two cultural roles that all urban places performed, although with varying degrees of intensity and elaboration.[9] Cities with predominantly *orthogenetic* functions serve as centers for the construction and codification of the society's traditions. In such urban places, cadres of literati rationalize a great tradition of cultural performance and ideology and disseminate it to society at large. The cultural

[7]Gideon Sjoberg, *The Preindustrial City, Past and Present* (New York: The Free Press, 1960), pp. 7-13; Oscar Lewis, "Urbanization Without Breakdown: A Case Study," *The Scientific Monthly*, LXXV, 1 (1952).

[8]Milton Singer, "The Expansion of Society and Its Cultural Implications," in *City Invincible: A Symposium on Urbanization and Cultural Development in the Ancient Near East*, Carl H. Kraeling and Robert M. Adams, ed. (Chicago: University of Chicago Press, 1960); Horace Miner, "The City and Modernisation: An Introduction," in *The City in Modern Africa*, Horace Miner, ed. (London: Pall Mall Press, 1967); Conrad Arensberg, "The Urban in Cross-Cultural Perspective," in *Urban Anthropology: Research Perspectives and Strategies*, Southern Anthropological Proceedings, Number 2, Elizabeth M. Eddy, ed. (Athens: University of Georgia Press, 1968); John Gulick, *Tripoli: A Modern Arab City* (Cambridge, Massachusetts: Harvard University Press, 1967); Anthony Leeds, "The Anthropology of Cities: Some Methodological Issues," in *Urban Anthropology: Research Perspectives and Strategies*, Southern Anthropological Proceedings, Number 2, Elizabeth M. Eddy, ed. (Athens: University of Georgia Press, 1968).

[9]Robert Redfield and Milton Singer, "The Cultural Role of Cities," *Economic Development and Culture Change*, III, 1 (1954), pp. 58-59.

message emanating from Banares, Bangkok, Washington, and other cities with heavily orthogenetic functions is to safeguard, sophisticate, and elaborate cultural traditions and stability. Cities with predominantly *heterogenetic* functions are centers of technical or economic change. Their cultural role depends on the creation and introduction of new ideas, cosmologies, and social procedures into the wider society. In cities like London, Marseilles, and New York, intelligentsia challenge old methods, question established traditions, and help make such cities the innovative centers of their societies.

Redfield, in his original formulation of the folk-urban typology and in his later work with Singer on heterogenetic-orthogenetic roles, introduced a significant and distinctively anthropological interest into the study of cities. Urban anthropologists who continue this approach (although they may disagree with the specific formulations) enjoy a strong conceptual framework for holistic research and utilize a diachronic orientation that entertains the many varieties of urbanism and urban people. The anthropology of urbanism has been most usefully and widely applied to urban places in traditional civilizations such as India, Southeast Asia, Latin America, and other formerly colonial societies now often identified as the third world. These cities and their societies are usually characterized by highly codified and long-standing cultural traditions. In earlier times these traditions were broadcast to the peasantry by literati resident in what Redfield and Singer would term heavily orthogenetic cities. The elaborated cultural traditions of such societies, their historical depth, lend themselves to the holistic, diachronic study that forms the basis for the anthropology of urbanism.

The present generation of anthropologists interested in urban places has been slow to follow the conceptions of Redfield and Singer. This situation came about because the anthropology of urbanism is weakest when the city is conceived as an amalgam of disparate groups, neighborhoods, economic classes, and political associations. The holism that led Redfield and Singer to emphasize the cultural roles of cities rests on the assumption of an urban homogeneity that discounts ghettos, unassimilated urban migrants, ethnic conflicts, and all the other behavioral and ideological disparities that define an urban center. Then, too, the intimate knowledge of a small and sharply demarcated social group or community, so often the anthropologist's trademark in primitive and peasant research, is diminished in the anthropology of urbanism. If the traditional intensive and small-scale research technique of the anthropologist in the field were maintained, how could this perception of a very limited urban segment generate an analysis of the urban whole? Especially as urban anthropologists confronted highly heterogeneous industrial cities, cities with rapid growth patterns, or cities formed by colonial domination (where traditions and cultural roles were intrusive rather than indigenous), they developed other conceptions and methodologies in their study of urban locales.

The Anthropology of Urban Poverty

The *anthropology of urban poverty* is another line of urban research pursued by anthropologists. It maintains greater continuity with traditional anthropological methods and the quest after the exotic than does the anthropology of urbanism, although it also thereby removes the holistic and cross-cultural approach from the scope of urban anthropology. Study of ghetto populations, urban ethnic subcultures, and poverty-induced urban social adaptations allows the traditional intensive and small-scale methods of tribal or peasant anthropology to be redefined in a city context. The poor in Puerto Rico and New York; urban alcoholic nomads along Skid Road, Seattle; streetcorner blacks in Washington, D.C.; and Amerindians throughout the United States[10] have all been subjects for this anthropology, which sees the city reflected through the ghetto and views urban man mirrored in the customs of the poor. The appeal of the ghetto approach to urban anthropology has been very great, not only because it promises methodological continuity with anthropology's traditional disciplinary style, but also because it offers a direct confrontation of the (activist) scholarly investigator with the sore spots of American, or contemporary, urbanism. This approach takes the city as a separate realm with its own dynamic within the larger society—specifically, those ghetto ethnics or urban alcoholics who are said to live out a skewed and twisted version of the society's goals or whose life-styles are described as being at the furthest cultural remove from the mainstream world.

Because it emphasizes both small, relatively closed urban social groups and urban lives under adverse social and economic conditions, the urban anthropology that studies the city via the ghetto often never moves beyond the poverty or ethnic enclave.[11] The social intricacies of ghetto life, the ideological framework of poverty existence, the nature of

[10]See Oscar Lewis, *La Vida: A Puerto Rican Family in the Culture of Poverty—San Juan and New York* (New York: Vintage Books, A Division of Random House, 1968); James P. Spradley, *You Owe Yourself a Drunk: An Ethnography of Urban Nomads* (Boston: Little, Brown and Company, 1970); Ulf Hannerz, *Soulside: Inquiries into Ghetto Culture and Community* (New York: Columbia University Press, 1969); Jack O. Waddell and O. Michael Watson, eds., *The American Indian in Urban Society* (Boston: Little, Brown and Company, 1971).

[11]Cf. Rollwagen, "Introduction," p. 003: "Since the subjects that [urban anthropologists] have studied often have been social groups *within* cities, they have not discussed the city within which their subject matter occurs."

disfranchised and outcast populations whose residence happens to be urban, generally assume larger scope than the city as such. The theoretical propositions of this urban anthropology thus concentrate more heavily on poverty and ethnicity than on the nature of urbanism. Many of its hypotheses serve to vindicate the anthropologist's concentration on the ghetto innards of the city. If ghetto inhabitants can be shown to be radically distinct from the urban mainstream then they warrant the singular attention of the anthropologist, much as did the self-contained societies of the Trobriand Islanders, the Kwakiutl, or the Nuer. Oscar Lewis believed that the urban poor live within a "culture of poverty" which exists (somewhat) autonomously from their economic and political deprivation and which conditions familial organization, belief patterns, and work behavior antithetical to the larger society's values.[12] The urban culture of poverty was to be the anthropologist's entree into the many disparate groups and activities that made the city impossible to study in a holistic fashion. Lewis's conjecture has been attacked on many levels: It substantially alters the anthropological notion of culture; it contradicts many qualities of ghetto life; it takes as codified and enculturated behavior in the ghetto what may only be a transitory adaptation to the harsh conditions of deprived urban existence; it comprehends only a small proportion of the urban poor (see Chapter Seven for more detail). At best, the concept is tied to contemporary societies and their urban patterns; at worst, it has become a poorly reasoned catch phrase promoting political passivity towards the poor.

Other anthropologists of the ghetto have also explored the conceptual framework that orients life among the urban poor or destitute. Although it too speaks of a "culture" of urban nomads, James Spradley's work on alcoholics indicates the different environmental references and life codes developed by inhabitants of skid row. Ulf Hannerz also follows this interest in an analysis of "soul" among Washington blacks and in an investigation of the adaptive strategies of urban ethnic groups striving for mobility in contemporary American society. The latter approach promises to make what the anthropologist discerns in the ethnic ghetto relevant to comprehension of the society as a whole, but it does so through a study of acculturation rather than urbanism (Chapter Seven presents these studies in greater detail). By striking deeply into the life-ways of the industrial city's downtrodden, these urban anthropologists build on anthropology's traditional strengths in small-scale research and pursuit of the exotic in continuing intensive and insightful studies of bypassed or economically deprived peoples and their life-ways.

However, Charles Valentine and others have suggested that full

[12]Lewis, La Vida, pp. xi-lv.

comprehension of the poor does not emerge from study in the ghetto alone, but from research among the rich and politically powerful as well.[13] Similarly, to talk of the cultural roles of cities, to put cities in cross-cultural perspective, to treat them diachronically as subject to fundamental change and variation, presumes a magnitude of insight and a degree of generalization beyond and outside the urban anthropology that perceives the city only from the urban canyons of its disesteemed and unvalued.

The Anthropology of Urbanization

Another urban anthropology comes from the contemporary large-scale physical movement of rural peoples to cities and the adaptations of these immigrant populations to the new urban environment. In the wake of these urbanizing peasants and tribesmen follow anthropologists, thereby traveling the scholarly path from village to city. Urban anthropology, seen as the process of urbanization, is especially strongly developed in African research (undertaken mainly by British anthropologists) and in Latin American studies (pursued by American scholars). Cities in these formerly colonial regions are characterized by high rates of rural outmigration, which has led in recent years to the spectacular urban growth (and equally explosive urban problems) that attract many urban anthropologists to the study of this process. In this urban anthropology, the city represents a distinct arena of social arrangements and life-styles to which the immigrant must accommodate at least so long as he interacts within the urban sphere. This *anthropology of urbanization* emphasizes the altered social structure, interpersonal ties, associational life, and ethnic or tribal identity that develop as tribesman or peasant becomes urbanite. Because the approach is microanalytic, specific aspects of the heterogeneous city—those related to its most recent immigrants—can be specified in great detail, often as a sharp corrective to accepted notions of the typical urbanizing experience. For example, the notion that urban residence inevitably leads to nuclear family patterns has been seriously challenged in several world regions. Tribal identities and associations (in altered form) appear not as useless ascriptive barriers for the new urban man but as important channels through which the new urban resident finds his place within the city.[14]

[13]Valentine, *Culture and Poverty*, p. 149.
[14]Lewis, "Urbanization Without Breakdown," p. 41; Abner Cohen, *Custom and Politics in Urban Africa: A Study of Hausa Migrants in Yoruba Towns* (Berkeley: University of California Press, 1969); Kenneth Lindsay Little, *West African Urbanization: A Study of Voluntary Associations in Social Change* (Cambridge: The University Press, 1965).

Urbanization studies often continue most exactly the nature of anthropology's traditional methods and units of study. Interest centers on a process—urbanization—and its consequences for human social existence, rather than involvement with a form—urbanism—and its relations to human society and culture. The nature of the urban locale— its cultural roles in society, its demography, class organization or government—stands as an unanalyzed or assumed backdrop for the more focused attentions of the anthropologist on urbanizing tribesmen and peasants. Anthropology's involvement with tribal society or peasant community has simply been transferred to urban locations as the anthropologist follows his informants from their rural homes to the city. Indeed, students of urbanization have often further refined investigative techniques originally used in tribal and peasant studies for application in urban environments. "Network analysis," which traces the many-stranded links between urbanites, and "situational analysis," which charts the social adaptations of the newly urbanized, have more fully rationalized old methodologies for the city context. These methodologies ultimately derive from the small-scale and intensive field methods of the primitive world.[15]

The difficulties that beset urbanization anthropology emerge from these very methodological continuities with past anthropology. The nature of cities cross-culturally and in historical perspective is difficult to see when the scholar deals with recently urbanized populations and *their* accommodation to the urban locale (rather than, as Leeds critically notes,[16] the accommodation of the urban locale to them). Field work undertaken in "native locations" or shanty towns also leads to a perspective that only sees the city by looking in from its very margins. Although convenient research units for the anthropologist, these locales are not the effective boundaries of social relations for recent migrants to the city. Urbanization studies try to avoid this myopic view by dealing with a "field of social relations" that may transcend the residential communities of newly urbanized people. But it is extremely difficult to build the complexities of the city and urban existence out of the multitudes of social networks in any urban center, and it is impossible to fit these into some larger view of the city in a diachronic and cross-cultural framework. Like the anthropology of urban poverty, therefore, urbanization anthropology specializes, both in conception and field technique, on

[15]Cf. J. Clyde Mitchell, "Theoretical Orientations in African Urban Studies," in *The Social Anthropology of Complex Societies*, Michael Banton, ed. (London: Tavistock Publications, 1966); also the various articles in *Social Networks in Urban Situations: Analyses of Personal Relationships in Central African Towns*, J. Clyde Mitchell, ed. (Manchester, England: Manchester University Press, 1969).
[16]Leeds, "The Anthropology of Cities," pp. 31-33.

studying a particular kind of urbanism—in this case, cities in developing nations—with a specific pattern of rural-urban relationship leading to high levels of migration to the city.

The three urban anthropologies discussed in this section accentuate different qualities of anthropology and therefore ask different questions about urban institutions. Each offers advantages for certain scholarly questions and in certain kinds of cities; each suffers limitations in concepts and problems of methods. A complete urban anthropology requires a combination of the urbanism, urban poverty, and urbanization approaches into a general framework for the analysis of cities. This book attempts to make such a combination by pursuing the anthropology of urbanism. This approach is most effective in treating cities of many varieties and periods. It can engender comparisons and analysis that will accommodate the insights and interests of the anthropology of poverty and the anthropology of urbanization without suffering from their limitations in method and conception. Indeed, the anthropology of urbanism enhances the other two urban anthropologies. It does so by indicating how different urban situations may lead to different kinds of poverty enclaves in the city and by denoting what sorts of urban conditions create rapid and large-scale urbanization. The following chapter outlines the specific approach to the anthropology of urbanism that will be utilized in this volume.

2

Cities
and Societies

To see the urban locale and its cultural roles within the larger society is the major goal of the anthropology of urbanism. Many scholarly fields, such as history, sociology, and city planning, emphasize the urban world as a separate social realm with its own dynamic and chronology. They note its unique features of heterogeneity, ecological zones, communication webs, and architectural forms. This perspective, which removes urban places from the context of their societies, may be appropriate to what these disciplines wish to learn of and from the city. Such an approach is less useful in anthropology, however. For cross-cultural comparisons and analyses of urban development, the city must be treated as only one of many social institutions such as kinship, religion, and subsistence activity that anthropologists always have conceptualized as parts of a socio-cultural whole.

This book sets forth two ways in which urban anthropologists may perceive the city in terms of its setting in the larger society and the cultural roles it performs. Both depend on a diachronic framework and a wider viewpoint than the single urban site or one of its component class or ethnic populations. One way is to focus on the ideological ties that bind a city to its society and vice versa; that is, to measure how the ideological motifs of the society are embedded in the culture of its cities, and to recognize how the urban locale projects self-generated beliefs onto its environs. This approach is no great innovation in anthropology. Is there any difference between studying belief systems as they affect carvings on a totem pole or as they arrange urban space (the physical pattern of the city) and condition urban values?

The ideological approach thus studies the "rules" that compose the cultural roles of cities and their societies. It investigates the derivation of these rules outside the city or their diffusion from the urban sphere into the cultural setting. Most often, ideological relations between city and society represent a one-way flow from innovating city out to a more traditional surrounding region. Islamic religion, for example, arose in the special urban mercantile context of the medieval Near East. Over a relatively short period, however, it spread to the Bedouin tribes of the desert, and then later (by way of conquest) to African tribal peoples and European and South Asian peasants. Other examples indicate that the transmission of ideology between city and society may run in the reverse direction. The persistence of lawns and ornamental gardens in urban and suburban America illustrates the re-creation of the rural in a city situation—or perhaps more specifically, the maintenance of the same ideology that lies behind an English country squire's park or American gentleman farmer's meadows in an urban environment where rolling lawns and formal gardens are reduced to postage-stamp plots. Another example is the preservation of rural caste ideology in contemporary Indian cities in spite of the fact that the modern urban sphere destroys or greatly alters much of caste's former behavioral significance.[1] Whether as purveyors of new beliefs or receptacles of old ones, cities are intimately linked by patterns of values and ideology to their societies.

The other perspective on urbanism followed in this book is an interactional one: The city is a socio-economic and political factor in the organization of the entire society. It is both product and producer of particular political alignments, economic sectors, and social structures. Just as kinship organization stands in a functional relationship to ecological factors, just as the form of the family reflects political and economic institutions in any society, so the city relates to the political and economic order in which it exists. The interactional approach thus treats cities as performers of cultural roles within the social organization of their societies. Like any other social institution, the city is one behavioral part of a larger system.

The objective of an interactional approach to cities and societies is to see the actual behavioral lines that tie the city to its social setting and determine its development and place in the larger society. Urban politi-

---

[1]Richard G. Fox, "Resiliency and Change in the Indian Caste System: The Umar of U.P.," *The Journal of Asian Studies*, XXVI, 4 (1967).

cal parties in the United States, for example, are tied to national political parties in a web of patronage, formal party offices, and fund collection. At certain points in the history of specific American cities, urban parties have been more or less intertwined with their national counterparts—at times refusing to be externally dominated, at other times attempting to impress their own demands on the party's national policies. Another instance of how the city interacts with its society comes from preindustrial times. Very commonly in the past, the city was an extension of the ruler's court; it was an imperial center wherein rule of the city and rule over the state were not separate. As we will see in later chapters, given this pattern of interaction between city and society, the extinction or decline of a dynasty also brought about the demise of its capital city. Whether in decline or development, whether as the capital of empires or the arena for local politics, the city is always interactionally linked and behaviorally influenced by its setting in a society.

The ideological and interactional roles and links between cities and societies are not unchanging. Therefore the concept of "adaptation" must be added to introduce a dynamic aspect. Cities are and always have been in a continual process of adjustment to their external socio-cultural environments. "Environment" in this context does not directly involve physical circumstances affecting the city, such as water supply, soil type, and rainfall average. Rather, a city's external environment represents the sum of all the social and cultural factors impinging on the city (some of which may ultimately derive from the physical environment because of those cultural rules that are technologically and ecologically determined). These social and cultural factors include political pressures, economic conditions, communication and transportation channels, and rural values that condition a city's "foreign" relations with the part of the society external to it (including other urban places). Such factors necessarily affect the course of urban development and internal urban social arrangements. "Adaptation to an external environment" thus refers to the changing pattern of ideological and interactional links between city and society over time.

This process of external adaptation determines in large measure spatial arrangements and social life within the city. The organization of urban government, class structure, and residential arrangements reflects the city's economic functions, political power, and communication lines as they develop over time and in conjunction with or apart from those of the larger society. This internal adaptation of cities in terms of their *interactional links* with the society can be discussed as the "functional organization" of the city, or "urban organization." External adaptation also conditions urban values, spatial arrangements, and life-styles through the ideological links between city and larger society. The ideological arrangement of urban space and life-style as determined by the city's adaptation to external socio-cultural factors can be referred to as the "ideological form" of the city, or "urban ideology." Later in this chapter we will attempt to specify the major external conditions affecting the ideological and interactional roles of urban places and to define the kinds of urban places that arise in adaptation to such changing external conditions.

The process of urban adaptation and its effects on urban organization and ideology provide a conceptual base for investigating the settings of cities in their societies through time. This diachronic perspective on urban development and change can be pursued in two different ways. In the first approach the chronology of a single urban place is arranged into periods that show significant alterations in the links of the city to its society. The second part of this book, which deals with urbanism after the advent of industrialization, adopts this approach to urban adaptation in an analysis of two American industrial cities and a colonial town in India.

The other way of seeing urban adaptation is to treat the city in a general sense, as a social institution to be found in many societies, with adaptive variations at different points in the past and in different parts of the world. Rather than dealing with the specific pattern of a single city, we look diachronically at the range of variation in adaptive pattern found in different sorts of cities linked to different sorts of societies. The first part of this book utilizes such an approach in analyzing the nature of preindustrial urbanism and the varieties of cities that emerged prior to world industrialization.

So often in the study of cities, the magnitude and diversity of urban phenomena become overwhelming. How to deal with the multitudes of cities which exist or have existed? How to perceive the uniformities of urbanism within the particulars of a thousand cities? The concept of adaptation helps to categorize the great variability in the nature of cities. We can view the adaptation of cities to the wider society through interactional and ideological cultural roles as creating both a primary and a secondary level of urban variation. Primary urban variability reflects the general or gross nature of the socio-cultural environment. Thus, different sorts of societies lead to different kinds of cities. Preindustrial cities (e.g., cities before the advent of Western industrialization) share certain general characteristics that differentiate them from all industrial cities because of their technological and economic base. Industrial cities similarly share certain characteristic economic and productive arrangements. Birmingham in England and Birmingham in Alabama share more common urban characteristics because of their adaptations to industrial environments than either would have shared with fourteenth-century London or second-century Rome. The nature of technology, polity, and economy in the wider society (as we will see in more detail after the city is defined later) therefore provides a means of differentiating cities into general types that constitute the primary level of urban variability. This book recognizes and analyzes five such general types: Regal-ritual cities, administrative cities, and mercantile cities arise as primary varieties of the city in various sorts of preindustrial societies; industrial cities and colonial cities constitute the primary urban forms found in industrial societies.

To recognize that different city types are associated with different kinds of societies is not to cover the full extent of urban variation. Within any (primary) urban variety, a range of (secondary) urban variation exists because specific cities follow divergent patterns of adaptation to the larger society. For example, in terms of primary urban variability, Chicago and Charleston, South Carolina, share many common characteristics and have developed in very similar ways because an American industrial environment is their common setting. But Charleston and Chicago differ in population, urban morphology, ethnic arrangements, extent of industrialization, class structure, and ideology as a result of their individual patterns of adaptation to the industrial world. To understand the full extent of urban variation, we must not only analyze the five types of primary urban variability but also discuss the range of secondary urban variability possible within each of the general types. The cross-cultural urban case material found in Chapters Three through Five permits generalizations about the extent and direction of secondary urban variability within preindustrial urban types. Unfortunately, the range of secondary urban variability in industrial times has not yet been adequately surveyed. Indeed, a major conclusion of this book is that anthropologists should direct their urban research more to this question. Given the available data, Chapters Six and Seven must deal in depth with the adaptive pattern of individual cities, and therefore can only suggest through several examples the variety of secondary urban arrangements to be found in industrial environments.

It may be helpful at this point to anticipate a criticism of the above viewpoint. The manner in which terms such as urban adaptation, ideology, and organization conceptualize the city may elicit the charge of reification. This criticism would run that an inanimate city, which has no life apart from the urban multitudes that compose it, has nevertheless been treated as a living thing—as adapting, as having external relations and internal functions, all of which resemble the attributes of an animate being. Even though this book gives the city such attributes, the author does not believe the city "exists" apart from its human masses. Treating the city as a whole above and beyond its inhabitants serves the same didactive purposes as does conceiving culture in a superorganic way. Such a holistic viewpoint entails what some scholars might regard as reification. No matter, for this procedure is not evil *per se*. It becomes so only when put forth in a metaphysical sense (that is, really believing the city is a living thing) or when it proves useless or misleading. On the former metaphysical point, the reader has already been warned that this book does not propound such a view. The latter judgment the reader must suspend until the end of this book, when he will be able to gauge the practical and scholarly utility of the approach to the city presented here.

Studying the adaptation of cities to their socio-cultural settings has more immediate dangers than that of reification. The diachronic investigation of the links between city and society might wrongly be taken as a rationale for individual city studies, which were little more than compilations of urban chronology: "Imperial Rome and Its Development," or "Agra in the Time of Jahangir." Chronologies of this sort rarely lead to cross-cultural urban comparison or general views of city development because they highlight the unique temporal events associated with particular cities. Such studies are perhaps the province of the urban historian, certainly not the realm of the urban anthropologist. Neither in the study of the adaptive development of single cities nor in an investigation of the varieties of urban adaptation is the goal a chronological portrait of a city or a comparison of several such chronological profiles.

What value lies in juxtaposing Paris in the eighteenth century with Allahabad in the twentieth or Athens in the fifth century B.C.? Unless a general formulation is made of the adaptive urban patterns these cities represent and into which the specifics of their chronological development can be fit, there is little value in such comparisons. To make studies of the variety and diversity of city adaptation relevant to cross-cultural comparison and generalization, we must have in mind a typology of urban places. We need, that is, a scheme that classifies cities into different types on an arbitrary but clearly defined basis and that utilizes a diachronic perspective to arrive at these types. The primary urban types to be distinguished in this book have already been mentioned. The utility of such a typology is that comparison can be made not solely between, for example, Imperial Rome and Medieval Agra. Larger categories of urban places can be compared, too, freed from any specific geographical (in the sense of locational) or temporal (in the sense of chronological) context. Thus we may categorize cities from very different (chronological) periods as occurring in similar (social and cultural) "times." Any typology of cities clearly depends on intensive investigations of particular cities and their chronologies as a source of data. However, it replaces what might only remain an individual city description or a collection of city descriptions, each in a single time and place, with the goal of a general perspective on the urban experience in all times and places. Rather than juxtaposing Chicago and Madras, we compare the types of cities these two urban places represent.

What are the benefits of this proposed typology beyond facilitating cross-cultural comparison? Indeed, what benefits accrue from cross-cultural comparison? One purpose is to develop a more adequate description and theoretically illuminating view of what cities really are. Are we to accept as meaningful the idea that cities cannot by definition appear in nonliterate societies, a view propounded by V. Gordon Childe and Gideon Sjoberg?[2] Are we to limit the term "city" to those locales where a corporate community makes its own laws, forms its own (municipal) government, and fields its own army, as Max Weber would have us do?[3] Are long distance trade and the formation of an urban bourgeoisie the true index of urbanism, as is the view of Henri Pirenne?[4] How do we deal with the contention of Gideon Sjoberg that all preindustrial cities were seats of empire and administrative centers containing the state ruling elite?[5] Finally, do we accept fully the view of the city often found in contemporary sociological literature on urbanization, that demographic characteristics and developmental potential form the definition of the urban center? The contending viewpoints listed above all either implicitly or explicitly categorize cities.[6] The virtue of the typology of urban places presented in the course of this book will be that it allows a criticism and analysis of each of the foregoing viewpoints along with a specification of an alternative one.

Another potential benefit of the typology will be the ability to analyze certain urban characteristics as they pertain to particular types of cities. Terms or concepts in common use such as rural-urban migration, rural-urban antagonism, and rural-urban distinctiveness all conspire to a single image of the city's role within the larger society. A

[2]Gordon Childe, *What Happened in History* (Baltimore, Maryland: Penguin Books, 1954), pp. 23-26; Gideon Sjoberg, *The Preindustrial City, Past and Present* (New York: The Free Press, 1960), p. 7.

[3]Max Weber, *The City*, trans. and ed. by Don Martindale and Gertrud Neuwirth (Glencoe, Illinois: The Free Press, 1958), pp. 54-55.

[4]Henri Pirenne, *Medieval Cities: Their Origins and the Revival of Trade*, trans. by Frank D. Halsey (Princeton: Princeton University Press, 1925).

[5]Sjoberg, *The Preindustrial City, Past and Present.*

[6]Another instance of this use of an implicit definition of a city is the common archaeological practice of denying true urban status to various sites with monumental architecture because they were "only" cult centers. While it may be important to distinguish such cult centers from other forms of urbanism, this distinction is often based on the archaeologist's implicit (and sometimes ethnocentric) assumption of what constitutes a city. For example, see Michael D. Coe, "Social Typology and the Tropical Forest Civilizations," *Comparative Studies in Society and History*, IV,1 (1961), pp. 65-85.

comparative viewpoint based on a belief that the urban experience is
varied, and yet that it can be categorized, will help avoid a monolithic
conception of cities. It will also avoid a stereotyped view of cities' internal
characteristics or their external relations with the larger society.

The typology of urban places developed in the course of this book
nevertheless depends on a recognition of the city as a cross-cultural type.
The city is a characteristic social institution to be found in historically
separate and geographically removed cultural traditions. Certain social
and cultural regularities are associated with its existence in any society.
The definition of the city to be utilized here details the nature and
characteristics of the urban locale within any social system. The classification of different urban types notes the significant (primary) variations and varieties of the city taken as a general type.

On what basis do we compose a definition of the city and construct
a classification or typology of cities? As in all such endeavors, the criteria
will be arbitrary, that is, at the discretion of the researcher, and chosen
according to what he deems significant for his research objective. The
foregoing pages have argued that the anthropology of urbanism continues the holistic scholarly traditions of anthropology in its approach to
the city. It emphasizes the interactional and ideological roles played by
cities in their societies. Logically, then, our definition of what a city is and
our construction of an urban typology must proceed from a holistic and
diachronic view of the roles and adaptations of cities in their socio-cultural settings.

CITIES AND STATES

Not all societies have cities. Just as the automobile would look out
of place in a society with a stone-age technology, so the city does not exist
in societies whose largest social unit is a band composed of several
nuclear families. Cities are found only in societies that are organized as
states. The complexity of the city as a social institution directly reflects
the complexity of state political and economic organization. The city is
thus defined as a center of population concentration and/or a site for the
performance of prestige and ceremonial functions found in a state
society. The links between city and society emerge from the cultural
roles —economic and political as well as ideological functions—that the
city performs within the state society. The pattern of external adaptation
linking city to society—and thus a holistic view of the city in its social and
cultural setting—emerges from investigating the ideological and interac-

tional ties of the urban locale to the state society. Different sorts of states (with varying technologies and urban economies) will have different types of cities, each with a distinctive urban ideology and organization and therefore a specific constellation of cultural roles. These differences underlie the typology of urban places that will appear later in this chapter.

What, then, is a state society? And how is the complexity of the state reflected in an institution—the city—unique to such societies? The state is a political institution found in those societies where coercive force and economic control are monopolized by a governing body. The term "state" sums up a particular form of social organization in which inequalities of power and wealth among people structure leadership and access to economic goods.[7] In primitive societies, internalized guilt, public shame, social ostracism, and kin feuds are the major ways of enforcing norms when the social order is threatened or broken. These methods are particularly effective in small, "face-to-face" societies. Such personalized and small-scale techniques of social regulation and enforcement of social mores place severe limits on the population, economic specialization, and political hierarchy that can still be effectively controlled. The state represents a very different answer to the problems of social control. It replaces shame, guilt, and kin feud with the force of regal or governmental decrees. These ultimately derive their power from the threat of physical force, economic expropriation, or political excommunication as wielded by the leaders of the society. The physical and economic power of state societies enables them to enforce social conformity over wider territories and greater numbers of people than any primitive society can do. State societies enjoy much greater centralized control over the productive process and more forceful curtailment of feuds and other strife, which can run unabated in the primitive world. Because the governing body or leaders of the state arrogate to themselves economic wealth and political preeminence, they usually act as managers of both the system of agricultural or industrial productivity and the political decision-making process. States therefore have high levels of productivity and a great degree of specialization. The term "specialization" not only refers to craft workers and artisans, but also denotes a political class of people who are set aside from subsistence agricultural or industrial production. They are freed to staff and manage the offices of authority that compose the governing body of the state society.

Cities are another institution dependent on the specialization possible in states. They stand apart from the subsistence activity of their rural

[7]Cf. Morton H. Fried, *The Evolution of Political Society: An Essay in Political Anthropology* (New York: Random House, 1967), pp. 227-42.

surroundings; they are the physical habitation of economic, political, and ritual specialists found only in state orders; they symbolize architecturally a different social world than that characterized by the mud huts and dirt lanes of rural villages. Such reflection by the city of the state is more fully analyzed later in this chapter.

A major distinction among state societies concerns the technology upon which they depend. Where human or animal labor forms the primary energy resource in the society, the state can be categorized as "preindustrial" in technology. This condition obtained in all state societies and their cities until the Industrial Revolution began in eighteenth-century Britain. Industrial technology—in which machines and fossil fuels represent the major energy resource—has increasingly characterized Western state societies since that period. Their industrial advantage allowed European states to dominate many preindustrial states of Asia, Africa, and the Americas during the eighteenth and nineteenth centuries. As their productivity was harnessed to the economies of their European colonial masters, these preindustrial states also participated in and were transformed by an industrial world technology (usually into suppliers of raw materials, including cheap human labor). Although the new states and former colonial dependencies of the third world do not yet fully enjoy industrial technology, their history of accommodation to colonialist industrial states, energy requirements, and technological goals all indicate that they must be assigned to the industrial category of state societies.

States also differ in the complexity, social composition, recruitment style, and degree of coercive force associated with the governing body. At their simplest, states may be organized around weak kings who have very limited powers of coercion over their followers and consequently whose material well-being duplicates the lot of the common man. More complex states have strong kings or emperors who rule in autocratic fashion and whose predilections to pomp and ceremony dramatize their considerable wealth and their removal from the condition of lesser men. In such states, bureaucracies form to which the ruler delegates the practical supervision of the government. At their most complex, states contain highly specialized governing bodies that depend upon a wide dispersal of the hegemony that is undivided in less complex states. Police, courts, parliaments, ministers, and presidents each control a segment of the monopoly of force and concentration of economic control found in such state societies.

In some states, access to positions of power and wealth is relatively open. Such is at least the model in popular democracies. In other states, rulership is determined by ascription; it descends as a matter of birth to the sons of kings or to scions of the reigning kin group. Whether as ascriptive kingdom or egalitarian bureaucracy, all states distinguish between those people who govern and therefore have power over others, and those who are subject to and follow the dictates of government.

Leaders in state societies usually enjoy higher status and greater wealth than the common man as attributes of their power and control over the destinies of the populace. In simpler states, status and economic goods intertwine in a redistributive model of rule. The rulers are necessarily rich because their political positions must continually be validated by feasts and ceremonials. Such ceremonies enhance the rulers' power as they drain away their economic substance. The populace benefits economically at times from the quest for status by the ruling elite. Under other conditions, the populace is made servile and oppressed in this pursuit of prestige. In either case, whether as gifts from obedient subjects or forced exactions from recalcitrant peasants, the goods and services needed to maintain the elite status of the ruling group are produced by the commoner population. In such states, wealth accrues to the rulers as a matter of their position: The leaders of the state are wealthy because they are the leaders.

In more complex states, especially industrial ones, where an impersonal market economy generates and distributes wealth, the ruler is removed from direct economic benefit from his political office. Indeed strong strictures exist against his profiting while in the service of government, as illustrated by the many scandals concerning mink coats, refrigerators, and farm subsidies in our own state society. In such states, however, wealth is often a prerequisite for government office. Because they are wealthy some individuals are able to become leaders. We have come to see this most vividly in late years in the rising costs of running for the United States Congress or the Presidency, expenses which all but debar any but the wealthy.

Because cities are part of their state societies, they also contain distinctions among individuals. This stratification is most evident when the city is also the royal residence or seat of empire. Then the various grades of society distinguished in the state are naturally also to be found in the capital. Even when cities do not house ruling personages, their internal organization still demonstrates the existence of different grades of society. In the early Middle Ages, cities of northern Europe had a predominantly mercantile character and were not the habitations of the rulers. Nevertheless, social distinctions were drawn in such cities between burgesses, or townsmen with citizenship, and those who were not. Such burgesses had preferential rights to political offices in the town, and the very wealthy among them often formed a small and closed

ruling clique, or urban patriciate. Their positions and power were similar, although on a reduced scale, to those enjoyed by landed princes and
other rulers of the rural countryside. That the social order of the city
directly or indirectly reflects the social distinctions found in the state is
an important indication of the links between city and society.

The city reflects the state society in still another way related to
social stratification. Just as kings rank above nobles, who in turn stand
above peasants, and just as counties give way to provinces and then to
nations as ever more inclusive and influential branches of government,
so cities and rural places form a hierarchy of (urban) settlements. The
most familiar sort of urban hierarchy to someone from an industrial
state society such as the United States is a rank order of urban places
based on industrial and commercial services. Taking the country as a
whole, we might speak of a primary grouping of major commercial and
industrial centers such as Chicago and New York, a secondary category
of regional centers such as Charlotte and Buffalo, a tertiary level of local
centers based on cities like Watertown and Springfield, and so forth until
all urban places formed part of the hierarchical scheme.

To understand cities in nonindustrial contexts, another sort of
urban hierarchy must be drawn. This one ranks cities not on the basis of
their transportation or communication nodality, but on their rank in a
hierarchic network of urban ritual status or political power. As will
become clear later, in many state societies, cities are arranged in a linear
order by their ritual significance or in terms of their government functions. For example, Banaras ranks as one of the most holy, if not most
holy, city in northern India, a position that reflects an urban hierarchy
based on ritual criteria. Perhaps the role of Washington, D.C., in the
United States is broadly similar if the extra-territorial quality of the city
(being part of none of the states and yet superior to all of them) is
emphasized. But the great dispersion of political, economic, and ritual
functions in this nation, the lack of an accepted urban hierarchy based
on religious symbolism, and the ultimate economic rationality of urban
institutions in an industrial society means that the significant American
urban hierarchy depends on commerce, communication, and industry.
The Washington baseball team left the capital city for greener fields,
because regardless of whether baseball constitutes the American ritual
sport, its persistence in a particular city depends on market factors in the
urban area and not the city's ritual significance. This example provides
insight into other bases of urban hierarchy when it is contrasted with the
pre-Columbian ballcourts of Mesoamerica that are invariably associated
with the most important ritual centers. Whether based on a hierarchy of
ritual status or on economic and commercial/industrial prominence, the
urban hierarchy links the individual cities of any state society into a

graded social pyramid. Such a pyramid is built up out of either ideological (ritual) or interactional (industrial and commercial) links.

The previous pages provide a definition of the city that equates it with a particular level of socio-cultural development, the state society. Because they exist only in societies organized as states, cities share or reflect many of the characteristics associated with such societies: They are abodes for power and wealth inequalities between individuals, participants in a functional hierarchy, and specialized institutions within the highly differentiated social order of a state society. Are cities and state societies equivalent? Clearly not; the other aspects of our definition will help define precisely how the city is different and demarcated from the wider society to which it is nevertheless indelibly linked.

TO SEE THE CITY

In the Middle Ages, few Europeans would have had difficulty in deciding what was a city and where it began and ended. The walls and gates of a medieval urban settlement effectively divided urban space from rural surroundings. Such ease of judgment of the city's boundaries cannot so readily be duplicated in urban industrial America. In the great span of cities that comprises the megalopolis of the Atlantic Coast from Boston south to Washington, where does a particular city or the urban in general give way to rural settlement? Does any open space, any patch of grass or plot of land devoid of factory, building, gas station, or traffic light, mark the end of the urban sphere and the beginning of the rural? Clearly, the limits of cities would be very difficult to mark in northeastern industrial America.[8] The same holds true at the opposite end of the urban scale: The simplest cities are not readily divisible from their non-urban surroundings. Before proceeding to a discussion of primary urban types, we must clarify how to pick out or locate a city or urban settlement as distinct from its social surroundings, and thus to indicate in what ways city and state society are not equivalent. To do so is to move away from the intuitive and therefore often ethnocentric judgment that is sometimes used to solve this problem: What looks like a city is or must be urban. But what looks like a city to an individual is heavily conditioned by the nature of cities in his native society. When we look beyond the limits of industrial urbanism, beyond our own ethnocentric

[8]Cf. Jean Gottman, *Megalopolis: The Urbanized Northeastern Seaboard of the United States* (Cambridge, Massachusetts: The M.I.T. Press, 1961).

markers of cement sidewalks and high-rise buildings, beyond personal alienation and secularism, how do we recognize a city?

The definition of the city as population concentration or ceremonial and prestige center helps provide the answer. Both in a demographic aspect and also through social and ritual activities, cities form a locationally (or geographically) demarcated social zone that is cordoned off from the surrounding state society. In their internal social organization (population concentration) and ideological functions (ceremonial and prestige centers), they represent more complex human settlements than their rural environs. Both urban social complexity and ideological functions often take a spatial form in complex edifices and street plan. Medieval European city walls provided a defensive shield rarely found in villages against external attack, as well as ideologically defining the limits of an urban community whose corporate character had few rural counterparts.

Some types of cities, as we will see later, are more sharply demarcated in organization or ideology than others, which slowly fade away into the nearby countryside. Whether sharply differentiated or not, cities' separation from the rest of society explains why some scholarly disciplines approach cities as institutions unto themselves. For the anthropologist, however, this separation is taken as a quality of the urban institution, varying with the nature of the state society into which it is set. In many societies ceremonial activities often take place at special grounds set apart from normal living space (for example in temples or shrines), and yet such ceremonies are integral to the social process and belief system for the entire society. So too cities may be demarcated from the surrounding society but still be an essential part of it.

The two extremes by which the city is demarcated from the surrounding state society are summed up in the two characteristics defined as urban: "Population concentration," and /or "ceremonial and prestige center." At one extreme, to see cities as population concentrations is to view them simply as more densely settled versions of the countryside with correspondingly denser aggregations of facilities. Cities coalesce the extensive webs of communication and transportation, of economic marketing and political lines of control that run throughout the entire society but are most aggregated and centralized in the urban sphere. To see the city in this manner is to view it in terms of urban organization— that is, by its concatenation of economic, political, and communicative qualities. Demarcating the city by its demographic and communication functions is easy for modern Europeans and Americans, for it is the common way in which we perceive industrial cities (even though over the last quarter century the city's functions and population have dispersed over wide areas forming megalopolises that often do not fit our traditional vision of what cities are).

At the other extreme—one that is furthest from Western industrial experience—cities may be separated from their societies by ideological functions (which are concentrated in the urban area). In this case, the city stands apart from rural surroundings by its possession of unique physical qualities or "look." The higher "density" of ritual and (political) prestige functions in the urban place determines that "look," and ideologically links the urban sphere with the larger society. Here we are viewing the city as a ceremonial and/or prestige center as distinct from any population density or position in a web of transport, communication, political power, or commerce. Ritual buildings, elite edifices, defensive walls, or even only oversize ceremonial huts and the sacred or ceremonial activities that they house form a physical and visual testimony to the city as a site ideologically apart from its environs.

All cities combine both ideological and urban organizational density in their separation from the larger society, a separation that at the same time underlies the urban cultural roles (or external adaptations) linking city with state society. Even in industrial urban places where the city as functional web and population concentration is most evident, ceremonial and political edifices, monuments, and activities mark the city off ideologically. In some American cities the necessities of urban ideology may actually hinder the organizational character of the city. In Washington, D.C., no building is allowed to rise higher than the Capitol, even though demographic exigencies might demand a curtailment of the Capitol's symbolic pre-eminence. In all American cities, the special status of the "Downtown" area is recognized as something different from the combination of businesses and offices often equally developed in the suburbs—a recognition, by the way, that often leaves this area as empty after dark as if it were only a city of ceremony or a site of ritual.

At the other extreme, whenever cities were mainly ritual centers, they were still receptacles of population to a limited extent. Their small coteries of priests or rulers and retainers were occasionally or seasonably augmented by masses flowing into the urban core for ceremonial events—the birth or death of a king, or the supplication of the divine. Even if mainly repositories of kingly or priestly status, such settlements performed some functions of communication: They were centers for the dissemination of sacred lore or the moral dictates of rulers. Thus, to see the city requires more than the demographic view of the industrial world and more than the sacred or kingly center view of the nonindustrial. Different sorts of cities found in different sorts of states are demarcated by varying amounts of demographic and communication aspects ("urban organization") on the one hand and sacred and kingly status ("urban ideology") on the other. Besides distinguishing different sorts of states and attendant cities, the urban typology that follows specifies which sorts of cities depend more heavily on urban ideology and which on urban organization for their separation from the surrounding society.

Cultural Roles and Primary Urban Types

If state societies are the social and cultural settings in which cities develop, if they constitute the primary environment to which urban places adapt, then a logical postulate is that different sorts of states will have distinctive sorts of cities. Their settings in different types of states profoundly affect the external relations and thus the cultural roles of cities. Although the specific urban functions, or cultural roles, performed by cities take place within the political and economic institutions of the larger society, they can be abstracted from their societal context to give some idea of their latitude and diversity. The cultural roles performed by cities are (a) ideological, (b) administrative, (c) mercantile, and (d) industrial. All cities perform these roles in varying degree, but under particular conditions, either the ideological, the administrative, or the mercantile-industrial can be viewed as the dominant or primary cultural role of cities in a specific society. These economic and political conditions and the urban variety associated with them are detailed in the typology that follows.

Before turning to the actual urban types and their associated state societies and economic institutions, we must clarify what each of these urban functions entails. The *ideological cultural role* is performed by the city when it functions as a center of cult and ceremony, a site of political prestige and regal functions (as distinct from bare political coercion and power), a stage for the enactment of rituals that buttress or even define the powers of the state elite—whether sacred priest, divine king, or bureaucrat-president. All cities, but especially capitals, are heavily involved with the trappings of ritual and prestige that legitimate the state and the ruling elite, that broadcast the social order as an aspect of the divine or at least the suprahuman, and that thereby charter the city as a center of belief and ceremony.

Administrative functions are performed by the city in its role as a concentration of political power, an abode for the elite who wield this power, and a storehouse for the economic wealth drained from the surrounding rural countryside by such power. Through its administrative functions, the city coalesces transportation and communication channels, dense populations subsuming both military-administrative elites and their servitors, and appurtenances such as walls, temples, palaces, markets, plazas, universities, and gardens. These appurtenances strikingly distinguish the puissant city from its economically, politically, and culturally denuded hinterland.

Mercantile functions are performed by the city in its role as a site for the production of wealth through trade, land speculation, and craft production (as distinct from revenue levies on the rural hinterland garnered through urban administrative functions). Here the city broadcasts a particular economic regimen to the larger society and also becomes a center for the supply of luxury and high status goods. The mercantile cultural role is generally undertaken by specialized urban merchant populations but may also include the administrative elite as capitalizers of trade or handicraft. Mercantile functions based on land speculation are usually in the hands of administrative elites.

Industrial functions are performed by the city in its role as a center for the creation of wealth in the society, but through industrial productivity rather than mercantile activity. Here specialized institutions of production and transaction—factories, stock markets, railroads, etc.—as well as the specialized institutions of government required to maintain them flow out from the city. They, in turn, transform the economic activity, organization of labor, and productivity in the wider society. In many respects, the industrial cultural role is like mercantile functions except that new technology and social organization make the city even more a producer of wealth.

Specifying these self-evident urban functions in itself says little that is new about cities. These urban functions or cultural roles must next be related to particular socio-cultural contexts: Under what conditions in the larger society is the urban administrative cultural role foremost? In what societal contexts do ideological functions predominate in cities? Since the city has been defined in terms of state societies, it follows that different concatenations of state power and organization will relate to the variable importance of a particular urban function. The economic autonomy of the city (in terms of wealth production) from the larger society is also an important dimension. These factors are not presented as necessarily casual, but they are advanced as useful in indicating the connection of particular urban functions with specific economic and political settings. The two dimensions to be used in typologizing the primary level of urban variability are:

1. Extent of state power. The important diagnostic of state societies, as discussed in the previous section, is the existence of a ruling body, or government, that exercises social control ultimately based on physical coercion. State societies can thus be categorized by the amount of coercion they can exercise on their populations. Coercion is measured by the

territorial extent and centralization of power associated with the state. Another (and complementary) means of categorizing states depends on the degree of specialization and organizational complexity of the ruling body: to what extent state leaders form an economic and political class set apart from the general population; to what extent access to power is determined by birth or achievement; and to what extent specializations of functions and bureaucratic organization exist within the ruling body. Based on these criteria (elucidated in subsequent chapters), state power may range from weak to strong—or in terms of organization, from *segmentary* to *bureaucratic*.

The cultural roles of cities also vary along this dimension of state power. In weak, or segmentary states, the ideological function of urban places is primary and defines the external adaptation of the city to the wider society. In strong, or bureaucratic states, the urban administrative function is most significant in defining the links of city and society.

2. Extent of urban economic autonomy. This dimension measures the degree to which the city is an independent producer of wealth in trade or industry and therefore the extent to which the economic organization of the urban sphere dominates and transforms productivity throughout the entire society. Such economic conditions may vary from the complete *external dependency* of the city on food and revenue drawn from its rural agricultural environs to total *internal autonomy* of the urban sphere in the production of wealth and in the determination of economic practices for the entire society. The greater the economic autonomy enjoyed by cities in state societies, the more developed will be mercantile or industrial urban cultural roles.

The two dimensions of state power and urban economy can be plotted as axes of a graph as in Figure 1. This representation postulates that specific combinations of state weakness or power and urban (economic) dependency or autonomy are related to the predominance of ideological, administrative, or mercantile-industrial cultural roles in cities. For example, the figure posits that urban ideological functions would be strongest when the state is segmentary and urban economy is externally dependent. Any empirical case might differ from this expectation depending on the specific nature of the individual city. Figure 1, however, attempts to classify a *primary* pattern of urban cultural roles under particular economic and political conditions, rather than to specify the secondary urban variability that makes every city within a state society somewhat different (see previous discussion, pp. 20–21).

To note how these urban cultural roles gravitate around particular combinations of state power and urban economy is not sufficient, how-

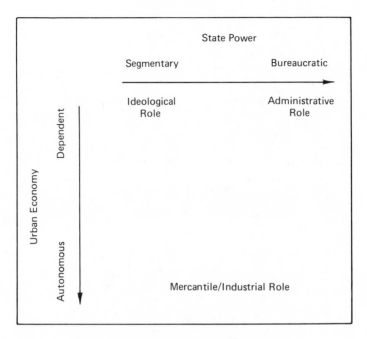

Figure 1. Dimensions of Urban Cultural Roles.

ever. They must be given a conceptual embodiment that can be used as a referent to analyze or comprehend empirical cases of state societies and their attendant urban forms. Figure 2 presents such a typology of urban places based on the foregoing cultural roles and the political and economic conditions of state societies that accentuate one or another of these roles. The five primary urban types in Figure 2 represent examples of the "constructed type": "a purposive, planned selection, abstraction, combination and (sometimes) accentuation of a set of criteria with empirical referents that serves as a basis for comparison of empirical cases."[9] Thus, on the basis of the typology illustrated in Figure 2, we should expect that under conditions of weak state power and high urban economic dependency, the ideological functions of cities will be primary in the society and that such urban places will have the characteristics of regal-ritual cities. When the state is strong and urban economy is autonomous, so that mercantile roles are foremost, we expect the character of cities to follow the mercantile type.

[9]John C. McKinney, "Sociological Theory and the Process of Typification," in *Theoretical Sociology: Perspectives and Developments*, John C. McKinney and Edward A. Tiryakian, eds. (Englewood Cliffs, New Jersey: Prentice-Hall, Inc., 1970), pp. 247-48.

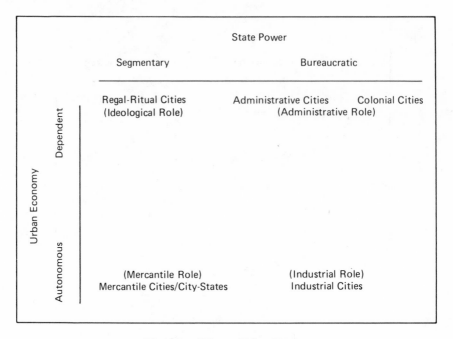

Figure 2.   Primary Urban Types.

Based on the definition of the city and the typology of primary urbanism previously provided, the following chapters delimit the different kinds of states in which specific urban types occur, the varying role of urban organization or ideology in city characteristics, and the relative dependence of different urban types on ideological or interactional links to the larger society. Case material on actual state societies and their attendant cities will be presented to elucidate the criteria behind each of the five primary (constructed) types and to indicate their usefulness in the explanation of empirical urban conditions.

The following chapters are divided into two major sections, according to the technological base of the state societies and cities under discussion. This division facilitates discussion of alternative urban typologies differing from that presented here; it also tends to correspond to the three urban anthropologies discussed in the previous chapter. Chapters Three through Five treat the nature of urbanism before the advent of industrialism in the Western world from a diachronic perspective. Such urban types have represented the major sources of material for the anthropology of urbanism approach. Chapter Three deals with regal-ritual cities found as royal households and ceremonial localities in states characterized by weak political centralization, dispersed power groups, and a minimum of economic differences among inhabitants. Such urban centers, as they are found in East and West Africa, pre-British India, Dark Age Europe, and elsewhere are almost entirely demarcated from the larger society by urban ideology, much as the states in which they are set cohere around the ritual status of the ruling group.

Chapter Four discusses another preindustrial urban type, the administrative city, and the formulations of Gideon Sjoberg concerning this sort of city. Although Sjoberg makes the mistake of regarding all preindustrial cities as being of this type, our discussion will indicate that it is found in conjunction with a centralized form of the state, sometimes known as a bureaucratic empire. Administrative cities are the residences of the state ruling elite and the centers of government operations. They are the locales in which products and services extracted from the rural peasants are converted into the sumptuous houses, the expensive clothing, and the fine living of a wealthy and powerful state ruling elite. State political power and rural productivity combine to form the urban zone, to define its organization and ideology, and to determine its birth and demise. Examples of this type of city and state society are drawn from the medieval Near East, seventeenth-century France, and Tokugawa Japan.

Chapter Five deals with the mercantile urban centers and city-states found in medieval cities of southern Europe, premodern Japan, Southeast Asia before the Dutch conquest, and other places where state weakness and urban economic autonomy combine to produce examples of this type. International trade and finance and speculation in commerce and land were important economic aspects of these cities. Such economic aspects had profound repercussions on the organization of social classes, the nature of urban polities, and the relations of the city with the state society. Because the urban locale was economically autonomous and impressed its own economic organization on its rural surroundings, and because mercantile cities evolved in a political vacuum or under conditions of anarchy, such cities often developed into autonomous states of a type known as a city-state. The discussion of mercantile cities and city-states will help analyze the urban typologies put forth by Max Weber and Henri Pirenne.

Chapters Six and Seven discuss urbanism in the period after Western industrialization. The primary urban types discussed in this section—colonial cities and industrial cities—are associated with the anthropology of urbanization and the anthropology of urban poverty approaches respectively.

Chapter Six analyzes a type of primary urbanism, the colonial city, presently found in the developing states of what is sometimes called the third world. These cities, like the "prismatic" states in which they lie, are an uneasy amalgam of colonial political institutions and traditional social and economic conventions. No longer traditional but not yet industrial, colonial cities exemplify in the urban context the strains in economic development, the social conflicts, and the novelties of politics which beset the underdeveloped nations of the world. An introductory section analyzes squatter settlements and over-urbanization in Peru, Brazil, and India as indices of the colonial city. It is followed by a detailed inspection of the development and present status of a colonial town in northern India.

In Chapter Seven, significant changes in urban pattern are charted through the chronology and development of specific urban places. To introduce and validate this approach, Chapter Seven begins with a review of the directions that the anthropology of poverty has taken in the study of industrial cities and their populations. It indicates why the valuable perspective on city and society that emerges from this work must be augmented by a holistic and diachronic approach. Chapter Seven then provides an example of this rather different approach to the anthropology of industrial cities. It describes the changing pattern of external adaptation and internal organization of two very different American cities—Charleston, South Carolina, and Newport, Rhode Island—and thus delimits the nature of two secondary urban varieties within (American) industrial urbanism. The chapter concludes with recommendations as to how the anthropology of urbanism and the anthropology of urban poverty might be fruitfully combined in the study of industrial cities and for the general enhancement of future research in urban anthropology.

3

Regal-Ritual Cities

The study of urbanization has been a major interest of social science research on cities. "Urbanization" refers to a physical movement of people from rural areas to cities. The concept also implies that the social and economic modernization of a society will develop as its cities grow and the percentage of urban population increases. Present urbanization is thus viewed as analogous to the situation in Europe in the eighteenth and nineteenth centuries. At that time the growth of cities and the urbanization of the populace were developments intimately connected with the emergence of a new economic order and a modern industrial state. Whether urbanization in presently developing nations will have the same consequences for economic development and social transformation is a moot point, discussed more fully in Chapter Six on the colonial city.

Another problem with the urbanization concept stems from the overriding importance it gives to the quantitative aspects of cities and how little it values their ideological functions. How many people does a city have? What is its rate of population growth? What are the facilities it has to handle population? How do different zones of the city provide services to different elements of the population? What sorts of transportation and communication lines tie the urban populace together? All these questions naturally emerge from the study of urbanization and accentuate the numerical or quantitative aspects of cities. Some scholars go to the extreme of defining cities in terms of such demographic criteria. They ask how large and densely settled a settlement must be before it can be called a city, or stipulate that a certain percentage of the population must be engaged in nonagricultural pursuits for a city to exist. Thus population, density, and other quantitative measures of the urban area become the city's most significant attributes.[1]

This viewpoint is clearly valuable for understanding cities in industrial societies, where size and density of settlement indicate the economic, political, and communication nodality a specific city enjoys. But outside the industrial type of city and apart from a social science that takes that city as a universal model, the emphasis on urbanization, size, and numbers in the definition of cities is less useful. Why need the size of a city or its density of population have anything to do with urban sacred functions or political prestige? Were industrial Chicago reduced to the size of Oshkosh, it would no longer be Chicago. But if Washington shrank in population, would it not still be the capital? No Hindu regards Banaras as an important city of pilgrimage because of its size alone, nor would fluctuations in population seriously impair its ideological function.

The emphasis on urbanization in social science often means that cities in other societies are evaluated mainly in terms of industrially-derived notions of population, density, economic concentration, and transportation nodality. However, if we wish to study what cities are without prejudice and preconception, we must reject purely quantitative notions about urban places. We must recognize that density and population are significant factors in urbanism, but that they are not the only or necessarily the most important criteria for deciding whether a human settlement is or is not urban.

This chapter analyzes a type of settlement with a very different urban cultural role from the one defined for the city by the concept of urbanization. Rather than concentrations of dense population, the human settlements described in this chapter are very small places, hardly larger than villages in their societies. Or they are "empty" sites where perhaps no one ever lived. Rather than being centers of communication and transportation, regal-ritual cities enjoy few such functions and exist with few technological facilities. Finally, rather than centers of modernization and modernity, of sophistication and secularism, regal-ritual

[1]Cf. the discussion of what is called the "expediential" approach in Paul Wheatley, "The Concept of Urbanism," in *Man, Settlement, and Urbanism*, Peter J. Ucko, Ruth Tringham, and G.W. Dimbleby, eds. (Cambridge: Schenkman, 1972), pp. 620-21.

cities are the embodiments of the sacred in society, either in the form of priestly ruling classes or in the person of a sanctified ruler.

Regal-ritual cities are so little removed or demarcated by urban organization from the rest of their societies that their recognition depends almost entirely on seeing cities in terms of urban ideology rather than any demographic component. Although they almost completely lack a quantitative urban aspect, and although they are marked off from the surrounding society in such limited organizational ways, regal-ritual places are socially demarcated centers of political and ritual status unlike the rural areas of their societies. They are habitations for the secular or spiritual leaders of the state, emblems of the society's power distinctions, and symbolic of its social complexity. They therefore embody significant urban characteristics.

The term "regal-ritual city" signifies the essential quality of these settlements: Their primary urban role is ideological. This cultural role emerges from the prestige and status of the state ruler or the cohesive power of state religious ideology. All cities have this ideological cultural role in varying degree. What makes the regal-ritual urban type distinctive is that its existence depends almost entirely on ideological functions.

SEGMENTARY STATE AND REGAL-RITUAL CITY

The form of state society in which regal-ritual cities occur (see the typology of primary urbanism in Chapter Two) is a decentralized one in which the monopoly of wealth and power by a central figure—king, chief, or priest—is limited. Subsidiary areas and regents—kinsmen of the ruler, royal appointees with local power bases, or autonomous self-made magnates—wield power and control regions in their own right and on their own terms. Such local authorities duplicate the power of the central ruler on a reduced scale and often owe only nominal obedience to his wishes. In general, the further away from the ruler a subordinate magnate is, the more he can rule at his own discretion. Such decentralized states have been called "feudal" in a European context, and this terminology is often exported to other societies. Others of these states—examples being the Swazi and Rajputs to be discussed in this chapter—are seen as "tribal" because corporate kin groups (clans or lineages) define the nature of the ruling elite. Whether kinship or a paternalistic system of feudal grants lies behind the decentralized political system is not significant in describing this type of state. The important facts are that power is dispersed and that the rule of the central figure is duplicated in type if not extent at many lower levels of state administration.

Rather than the terms "feudal" or "tribal," a more adequate conception of these polities is embodied in the term "segmentary state," as proposed by Aidan Southall, or "theatre-state," as suggested by Clifford Geertz.[2] These states are segmentary in that they widely disperse power over various units and subunits: central rulers and subordinate rulers, capitals and provinces. The term "segmentary" also signifies the importance of kinship groups or pseudo-familial paternalism in the constitution of these states. The concept of "theatre-state" accentuates a different but complementary aspect of their social organization. The central ruler is a symbolic embodiment, a model or image of the state society; he concentrates in his person and household symbolic attributes of rule that are duplicated by lesser chiefs and rulers down the scale of state organization. The absence or lack of political centralism that makes these states segmentary also means that the ritual, prestige, and status aspects of the state loom large in its cohesion.

Another characteristic of this type of state society is that access to positions of authority ideally derives from heredity or ascription. As we will see, the royal clan of the Swazi provides the rulers for the state; the proper heir of Charlemagne is his son. This ideal is often abrogated by the harsh reality of the political process and the competition for power endemic in such weakly centralized states. Yet even local magnates who owe their preeminence to physical usurpation request the accolade of the king. Even if, in Southeast Asia, the old dynasty is deposed, the new ruler who sits in the regal-ritual capital quickly becomes a hitherto-unknown reincarnation of the divine. The symbolic aspects of rule thus continue even though the actual leadership of the state society changes. In state societies where centralized power is limited, the ideology of kinship or the divine nature of rule stabilizes the framework of political organization even if its personnel undergoes frequent changes through revolt and usurpation.[3] As we will see, the importance of the ritual status of the ruler is reflected in the ideological cultural role of the capital city or prestige center.

The organization of the Swazi, Rajput, and Carolingian state socie-

---

[2]Aidan W. Southall, *Alur Society: A Study in Processes and Types of Domination* (Cambridge: W. Heffer & Sons Limited, n.d.), pp. 248-49, and Clifford Geertz, "Politics Past, Politics Present: Some Notes on the Uses of Anthropology in Understanding the New States," *Archives Européennes de Sociologie*, VIII, 1 (1967), pp. 8-10.

[3]Fred W. Riggs, *Thailand: The Modernization of a Bureaucratic Polity* (Honolulu: East-West Center Press, 1966), pp. 65-88, and Robert Heine-Geldern, "Conceptions of State and Kingship in Southeast Asia," *The Far Eastern Quarterly*, II, 1 (1942), pp. 15-30.

ties chosen for analysis in this chapter is exemplary of segmentary political systems.

The Swazi State

The Swazi are a Bantu-speaking people who entered their present territory in Southeast Africa late in the fifteenth century.[4] The state society that emerged from Swazi conquest was highly decentralized, and economic wealth and political power were widely dispersed. Kinship is an important determinant of the social organization of the Swazi state. The chief and most of the ruling elite came from the Dlamini or Swazi "royal" patri-clan. Although the chief, who inherited the position from his father, was the symbolic head of state and ritual focus of government, his powers were far from absolute. Instead, all members of the royal clan enjoyed high rank according to their genealogical closeness to the chief or former chiefs. The numbers of such people were greatly swelled because the Swazi practiced polygyny—the higher a man's rank the more wives he had and consequently the more high status offspring he begot. Those closest in rank to the reigning chief were his siblings, uterine half-siblings, and uncles, and then in descending order depending on genealogical proximity came various degrees of what we would call cousins. The organization of the state ruling body thus arose from the kin segmentation of the royal clan (with the addition of other subsidiary chiefs who descended from conquered groups but whom the Swazi had left in power).

Just as the kin system dispersed high status over many clan members, so the territorial organization of the Swazi state decentralized political control away from the chief. Land under Swazi rule was divided into principalities or provinces, each of which was governed by a subsidiary chief, or chieflet.[5] Chieflets were either members of the "royal" clan or descendants of indigenous leaders left undisturbed by the Swazi conquest. Although in theory all power and governance emanated from the chief, in fact chieflets acted quite independently in their local jurisdictions. Each of these subordinate chieflets enjoyed powers, status, and economic wealth similar to the paramount chief's although on a reduced scale. In their rule and prestige, they were small-scale duplicates of the royal figure and stood midway between commoner and chief. Many of

[4]The following materials on the Swazi are derived from Hilda Kuper, *An African Aristocracy: Rank Among the Swazi* (London: Oxford University Press, 1947).

[5]This terminology follows that used by Southall for the Alur segmentary state, rather than the terms used by Kuper for description of the Swazi.

these chieflets were half-brothers or younger full siblings of the reigning chief, who purposefully had given them independent principalities to remove them as a threat to the stability of the chiefship.

Neither the chief nor his high ranking kinsmen formed a privileged wealthy class in Swazi society. They perhaps had more cattle and wives than common people, but their life-style was qualitatively similar to the mass of the population. The Swazi believed good chiefs should not stand apart or live differently from the rest of society; they were expected to practice the same customs, hold similar beliefs, and live at the same level as anyone else. The chief wore the same clothing as a commoner, and he followed the advice of the local proverb to the effect that a good chief does not flaunt his status. Rather than material goods or life-style, ritual observance and status etiquette distinguished chiefs and chieflets from their followers. Men sat at a distance from him because his presence was powerful; women did not look him directly in the eye because he was too symbolically potent to be treated as a familiar acquaintance.

Rajputs

In many parts of northern India before the British conquest—especially in the contemporary regions of Rajasthan and Uttar Pradesh—the Rajputs formed a class of local rulers.[6] Rather than having been dominated from a single center and by a sovereign ruler, Rajputs formed many separate state societies. These states have sometimes been called tribal and at other times feudal. Although such terms are often misleading and ethnocentric, they do point to the Rajput states as decentralized segmentary polities wherein power was dispersed and wealth differentials were minimal.

Each Rajput chief ruled over a varying amount of land settled by members of his own kin group or by those people whom he and his close agnates had successfully conquered. Below the main chief in a Rajput state came lower ranking kinsmen who were subsidiary rulers in sections of the domain. As in the Swazi state, the rank of the elite (ideally) depended on their genealogical connection to the founder of the state or the present chief. Also as in the Swazi case, the subsidiary rulers under

---

[6]More details on Rajput political organization and urban centers can be found in Richard G. Fox, *Kin, Clan, Raja and Rule: State-Hinterland Relations in Preindustrial India* (Berkeley: University of California Press, 1971), and "Rajput 'Clans' and Rurban Settlements in Northern India," in *Urban India: Society, Space and Image*, Richard G. Fox, ed. (Durham, North Carolina: Program in Comparative Studies on Southern Asia, Duke University, 1970), pp. 167-85.

the chief often enjoyed great autonomy in political and economic matters, and very often they established or attempted to establish their
independence from the chief.

The Carolingian State

The state ruled by Charlemagne in the European Dark Ages was
the decentralized sort also found among the Swazi and Rajputs.[7] The
economy of the "empire" was based on self-sufficient and largely autonomous landed estates, the owners of which formed an elite class. These
local magnates did not owe their property or status to Charlemagne. At
most they wanted the approbation of the king to enhance or solidify
their local positions. Counts presided over the regional administration of
the state. They were in theory appointees of the king and held their
positions at his will. However, since they were drawn from the ranks of
the local magnates, and since they were given land grants as compensa-
tion for their services, such counts quickly built up a local power base
and came to regard their offices as heritable possessions. As one moved
progressively closer to the boundaries of the state, Charlemagne's power
gradually diminished in favor of the almost autonomous local authorities. Similarly, the king's justice was increasingly replaced with feuds
based on kin obligations towards the outlying districts of the state. The
local magnates and their vassals formed a professional military class only
nominally under the direction of the king.

URBAN ADAPTATION

The adaptation of regal-ritual cities to the larger society reflects the
nature of segmentary states. The links of such cities to each other as well
as their ties with the general population heavily depend on shared
ideology and emulation of the ruler's prestige. A shared ideology and
status emulation work both outward from the regal-ritual city to the
surrounding society, and inward from the hinterland to the city. In the
former case, elements from the larger society play a major role in
defining the nature of regal-ritual urbanism. This ideological continuity

[7]Materials on Charlemagne and his state come from Peter Munz, *Life in the Age of
Charlemagne* (New York: Putnam, 1969).

may flow outward from the regal-ritual city to the countryside. In these cases, ideological elements of the premier or capital city influence the nature of settlement throughout the society. The extent of this duplication or continuity of motifs depends on the relative status of a specific regal-ritual city and the relative political prestige of its elite residents. Emulation of the attributes of the capital city can continue down to the simplest village and homestead. In ancient Siam, for example, the village headman was the lord of the village in a fashion similar to the king as lord of the state.[8]

The emulation of status and the shared ideology between capital and countryside form a settlement hierarchy in segmentary state society. This hierarchy depends on ritual status or political prestige. Those people and their places of residence that are most near the king or priestly ruler have the most ideology and attributes in common with his capital. The capital city and other regal-ritual centers therefore do not stand sharply demarcated from the rest of society; they are only the most concentrated localities of the ritual and status that mark all of the society to greater or lesser degree. Just as the power of the segmentary state ruler is abridged by secondary and tertiary political figures who exercise varying amounts of autonomy in their localities, so the capital regal-ritual city shares its significance with other cities, which descend in ever-decreasing splendor as images of the premier locale. Just as the position of the ruler depends heavily on the ideological aspects of kingship or on heavenly forces, so the presence of regal-ritual cities depends on a gradient of status that attaches to particular locations.

No rural-urban antagonism or rural-urban dichotomy in belief and behavior characterizes such societies. Residents of the regal-ritual cities are not different and detached in wealth, prestige, and ideology from the larger society or rural populace. They are simply *more* wealthy, prestigious, and powerful. Most importantly, the political and ritual roles of the residents in the capitals provide a model of the proper political order and status hierarchy throughout the otherwise weakly cohesive state society. Kings or chiefs may be deposed and their particular capitals may become empty of the status that gave them life, but other rulers emerge and their capitals in turn receive the ritual status and preeminence that once belonged to another place. Ideological links between the capital and the society, unlike these ties of actual power, survive to be redefined in a context new in personnel but traditional in cultural form.

The adaptations of regal-ritual cities to their setting in segmentary

---

[8]Heine-Geldern "Conceptions of State and Kingship," p. 20.

states is clearly seen in the Swazi, Rajput, and Carolingian urban pattern.

Swazi Royal Centers

The capital homestead of the Swazi chief and his royal centers constituted the regal-ritual cities in this society. In size, these regal-ritual cities were little different from a commoner's household; indeed their pattern duplicated a typical Swazi homestead in all but dimensions (the chief's homestead was bigger). But the capital and royal centers were symbolic locations, and they stood apart or were separated from common residences by their ideological and prestige functions and their use as the chiefly residence.

A commoner's homestead consisted of a cattle byre or enclosure to contain the family herds, a "Great" or ceremonial hut, barracks for unmarried sons of the household, and dispersed huts for the women and their married sons. The homestead was supervised by a headman, the husband of the several wives who comprised the household, the father of its married and unmarried males, and the supervisor of its economic and political life. Near the cattle byre stood the Great Hut, which was decorated with the skulls of cattle sacrificed to the headman's patrilineal ancestors. The mother of the headman looked after the Great Hut, which was ordinarily taboo to his wives. The barracks for unmarried sons guarded the entrance to the homestead and consisted of several nearby huts often located on either side of the cattle byre and surrounded by a strong wall of branches.

Between the barracks and Great Hut were the quarters for the wives of the headman and his married dependents. Each married woman, after a time of training under the headman's mother, was given her own hut and yards. These often were surrounded by a high reed fence. Here a woman raised her children, and here the headman visited his wives. To prevent quarrels between wives and to provide more adequate space, the homestead was often broken into several sections that were contiguous but spread over a wide area. The section in which the mother of the headman lived was called the "capital," a very significant point that links the commoner household with that of the chief, as will be clarified below.

When a headman died, he was succeeded by one of his sons, whose mother then became the new supervisor and guardian of the Great Hut. The new headman sent one of his wives to each of the sections of the homestead in order to maintain the family line.

The chief's homestead was the commoner one writ large. The major difference was that the territorial dispersion of the royal sections of the homestead was so great that each section formed a new settlement, called a royal "village" or center. What we see is a change of scale, but not a change of form. The most important regal-ritual city was the royal capital of the chief. Each Swazi ruler built a new capital, a process described later. Thus regal-ritual cities spread not as the result of economic or communication nodality, but through the biological life cycles of the Swazi rulers.

The capital of Swaziland consisted of the three main elements found in a commoner homestead, only greatly elaborated. The cattle byre of the capital was the largest in the entire state society. One end of the cattle enclosure contained a sanctuary where the chief was ritually doctored to increase his symbolic strength as a ruler. Near this sanctuary was a group of huts, all of which were referred to as the Great Hut, and which formed the residence of the headman's mother. One of the constituent huts served as the national shrine and contained ritual heirloom mats and other symbolically important goods. The national shrine hut was enclosed at the rear by a high reed fence that served as a place of concealment for sacred objects associated with the chiefship. In the national shrine hut the chief and his mother addressed ancestral spirits and performed rituals for rain, councillors gathered to discuss national problems, and the members of the ruling clan came to resolve family matters. This hut also served as the sleeping place for the chief's children, although only the mother of the chief could enter it. The other huts which formed the Great Hut were used for cooking, sleeping, and storage of grain or ceremonial objects. The Great Hut complex of the capital was much larger than corresponding huts in a commoner homestead because of the greater number of children in the large polygynous household of the chief. Yet the spatial organization and ritual functions performed by the Great Huts of commoner and chief differed only in elaboration, not in basic form.

Surrounding the Great Hut complex were two semicircular rows of huts belonging to officials of the state society. The inner row (closest to the Great Hut) was inhabited by men of very high rank who officiated in national rituals held in the capital. Others of these huts were inhabited by the retainers of these men. At either end of the outer semicircle lived the supreme civil administrator of the state and the supreme military commander (both appointees of the chief). Because almost every high ranking Swazi visited the capital periodically and often spent long periods in it, several hundred people and many huts were crowded into these semicircles. When an important Swazi was absent from his residence at the capital, he usually left one of his wives to maintain his hut.

On either side of the chief's cattle byre came the barracks or male dormitories wherein the men assigned to guard the capital lived. These barracks were much larger than their equivalent in a commoner household. The population of the chief's capital thus consisted of retainers, wives, the chief's mother, and state officials. Several hundred people, therefore, comprised the resident population of the largest regal-ritual city in Swazi society. Only in the annual state ceremonies did the capital become a great population center, increased by the flow of Swazi commoners in from the villages to see ritual performances.

Other chiefly centers existed, although they lacked most of the ritual buildings and social complexity of the capital. Such centers grew up in several different ways. The Swazi custom was for the chief to leave the capital under the supervision of his mother and to live elsewhere. Each chief built a subsidiary ritual center that operated as a predominantly symbolic administrative and military headquarters for the Swazi state. The administrative center lacked many of the ritually important huts and articles found in the capital, and also it did not contain the chief's mother or the chief's ritual wives. For these reasons, it was second in prestige and ritual importance to the capital city. Even lower in ritual significance were the many other chiefly places scattered throughout Swaziland. These ritual centers were simpler and had fewer state functions than either the capital or the administrative center. Indeed, they were hardly different from commoner homesteads in organization, although they were all considered to be places endowed with the prestige and power of the chief. To create a new settlement, the chief had only to send out one of his wives along with some retainers to establish a chiefly compound in some part of Swaziland or to reinvigorate a center that had once been important under a former chief. Such chiefly centers were thus more socially elaborate and geographically dispersed versions of the spacing of wives and their children characteristic of commoner homesteads. Nearby commoner homesteads and chieflets' villages were linked to these chiefly centers. They were, in turn, linked to the administrative center and capital in a rudimentary and mostly symbolic urban hierarchy.

The political cohesion of the Swazi state heavily depended on the chief's prestige being shared in ever smaller amounts by kinsmen, chieflets, and commoners. Similarly, the links that bound the chiefly centers with chieflet villages and commoner homesteads formed a hierarchy of regal-ritual centers based not on size and facilities or economic and communication nodality, but rather on a descending scale of ritual and symbolic political functions. The striking fact about regal-ritual centers in Swazi state society was their origin and definition by ideological and kinship factors rather than communicative, commercial, or political

power nodality. As old chiefs died and new ones replaced them, different capitals formed. As the chief married he built new centers.

Rajput Forts

The regal-ritual cities of the Rajput chiefs were physically over-
grown villages with the addition of important functions relating to the
maintenance of the chief's prestige and power. They were usually small
(from several hundred to ten thousand people) and functionally simple,
although some of the largest centers reached a much higher population
and thus formed "administrative cities" of the type we will discuss in the
next chapter. Rajput regal-ritual cities were originally roughly hacked
out of the bush by the chiefs as strongholds against attack from other
chiefs, dissident kinsmen, or the bureaucratic empires (see Chapter
Four) that periodically arose in this area of India and infringed the
authority of local kin rulers. Because of their military and protective
functions, Rajput regal-ritual cities at their simplest consisted of a mud
fort, often surrounded by moats and protective hedges or by consciously
cultivated dense bamboo groves. At their most complex, ornate "castles"
with even more developed military construction were built, and were
surrounded by temples, wells, artificial ponds, or other specialized architecture testifying to the power and prestige of the chief. The size and
complexity of these regal-ritual cities varied with the status of the chief
and the extent of his domain.
    The population of Rajput cities consisted of the chief, his close
kinsmen (minimal lineage), and other members of his kin group, as well
as agricultural tenants and retainers. Agricultural pursuits and warfare
were the main activities of such cities. This fact, in conjunction with the
web of kinship defining the leadership of such regal-ritual places, meant
that occupational diversity, ethnic heterogeneity, impersonality, and
secularism were for the most part absent from them.
    The list of traits given above indicates that an urban quality based
on size, diverse functions and facilities, or heterogeneity did not appear
in the chiefly centers. In what way were they regal-ritual cities rather
than simply rural villages? Rajput chiefly settlements were the ideological and physical centers of lineage independence, much as the capital of
a kingdom or empire is. Here the chief who led his kin militias into battle
resided. Here the kinsmen living in surrounding villages could repair
for protection or succor in times of need. Just as the chief stood above
his kinsmen in prestige and influence, so his regal-ritual city was an
enclave of status and functions different from and superior to the typical
village. Often the chiefly settlement was the religious center of the

lineage and contained the deity worshipped corporately by the chief and his kinsmen. Specialized construction such as temples, artificial ponds, and of course the mud fort marked off the chiefly area from the country-side. The chief and his close kinsmen often possessed kettle drums, horses, armed retainers, fine clothing, fancy dwellings, Brahmanic ritu-als, and other sumptuous commodities and status insignia that marked off their regal-ritual habitation from that of their rural kinsmen.

Because the chief required such specialized services and luxurious goods to maintain or elevate his status, the regal-ritual city was often a haven for a limited number of craftsmen, ritual specialists, and trades-men. The chief commonly endowed a market in his abode, guaranteed commercial safety not to be found in rural areas, and provided induce-ments for merchants to settle. The merchants and markets contained in Rajput centers more nearly resembled refugee camps than permanent commercial communities. Such was the case not only because the trades-men came together helter-skelter to enjoy the "peace of the chief." It was also the case because the Rajput leaders created the markets for reasons of status maintenance rather than commercial necessity. When the pow-er of the chief or his kin group waned, so too did the markets they created suffer a decline.

The above catalog of the services and activities of Rajput regal-ritu-al cities clearly indicates their political and status nodality within a rural area defined by kinship, and also their importance as market places of a low order to serve the chief and the rural populace. In terms of military and protective functions, market activities, ritual functions, chiefly resi-dence, and role as craft and luxury centers, such settlements stood much above and beyond the rural villages that surrounded them. They did, however, fall far short of duplicating the goods and functions that we commonly associate with the city.

Charlemagne's Castles

Like the Swazi chief, Charlemagne had many royal castles spread throughout his domains—although in the European case, multiple wives and marriages were not the reasons for the multiplicity of these sites. These royal castles and especially the most important capital of Aix-la-Chapelle constituted the regal-ritual cities in Charlemagne's state. The royal castles were more elaborate than the castle of an average magnate, although they bore strong resemblances to the latter, just as Swazi homesteads are smaller versions of the king's capital. These royal castles were the ritual centers of the state as well as the habitations of the state ruler. Their populations show a disposition of roles and occupations that mirror the symbolic status and ideological functions of regal-ritual cities in Swaziland and Rajput India.

At Aix-la-Chapelle, Charlemagne set out to build a new Rome. Even though the results bear little resemblance to the urbanism of the classical world, Rome, in an ideological sense, provided a model upon which to base construction of the capital. Several of the buildings were named after Roman originals and arranged around a central square in a conscious duplication of the Roman urban pattern. Christianity, in the form of a royal chapel and other ecclesiastic buildings, was another ideological component of Charlemagne's capital. The internal layout of the chapel most clearly reflects the role of ritual center played by Aix-la-Chapelle. Inside the chapel, persons of different status worshipped on different levels. At ground level, servants assembled before the altar of Mary; on the first floor gallery, magnates gathered around the king's throne and worshipped before the altar of Christ; on the highest level, a golden mosaic of God covered the ceiling of the cupola. The organization of the chapel symbolized in spatial and ritual terms the social organization of the kingdom. The heavenly city was at least symbolized if not physically realized in Charlemagne's regal-ritual capital.

Unlike the state buildings, which were built of stone, the domestic structures in which Charlemagne, his family, and his retainers lived were all made of wood. The grandeur of Aix-la-Chapelle and other royal castles did not serve primarily administrative or political purposes, which could easily have been undertaken in wooden buildings of the sort used as the royal residence. Majestic architecture served the prestige and ritual functions we have identified as typical of regal-ritual cities.

The population was more differentiated in Charlemagne's capital than their equivalents in Swazi and Rajput state society. The officials of the capital included the constable, cellarer, marshall, chamberlain, and custodian of the gate. These functionaries were to be found on all landed estates including those of the local magnates. In Charlemagne's time, however, two special officials acted for the royal center, and they formed the beginnings of a specifically nonrural administration. The court palantine was a secular magnate who presided over a special tribunal that met in the royal palace. The chancellor was a churchman, usually a bishop, who administered the writing office, or royal chancellory. Besides officials, Charlemagne's court attracted scholars, religious dignitaries, and visitors from foreign lands who gave the capital a cosmopolitan flavor. Charlemagne's ideological position as a leading ruler in Christendom brought him many gifts, including a white elephant from Harun al-Rashid, that made his capital a repository of the world's products—a quality found in modern cities only as a result of their commercial functions. The population of Aix-la-Chapelle was more specialized than other regal-ritual cities and was predominantly bound to the king as members or officials of his court, as suppliers of the court's wants, and as ritual specialists instructing him in religion or the scholarly knowledge of the times.

URBAN ORGANIZATION

The internal social organization of the regal-ritual city consists of simply the social arrangements of the king's court or the priest's temple, as the earlier material indicates. No independent municipal government exists specially to govern the regal-ritual place; a court functionary perhaps supervises proceedings in the capital. No defense force exists specifically for the regal-ritual city; the army of the king (which is no more than his armed retainers) is also the bodyguard of his capital. The population of the city consists of those bound to the court by kinship, official duties, or craft specializations. The ruler is surrounded by family and other kinsmen, by court officials, servants, ritual specialists, artisans, and others whose presence is solely a reflection of the ruler and his court. The numbers of such dependents and their specialization in occupational roles vary with the status of the ruler and the rank of his city in the regal-ritual hierarchy. Because of their nature and population, such cities are abodes of consumers, not of producers in a material sense, and therefore regal-ritual places are economically dependent on their rural environs. The product of the capital is an image of an ordered state rather than an industrial commodity.

The way of life in regal-ritual cities also grows out of the nature of the court or ceremonial complex. The life-style is defined by the calendrical round of state rituals, kingly ceremonies, coronations, funerals, preparations for war, royal feasts, and divine sacrifices, rather than by individualism and secularism. The resident population are the major practitioners and the high status participants in this round of rituals, which ideologically reinforce the role of the regal-ritual city as an image of the state.

Only in such annual or periodic state festivities and ceremonials is the regal-ritual city filled with many people. Only occasionally then does it achieve the other urban characteristic of population concentration. Why is the demographic, or organizational, urban aspect only periodic and of short duration in such centers? Again the explanation lies in the nature of the segmentary state and its reflection in the regal-ritual city. Just as the rulers of these decentralized states cannot concentrate great

power and wealth given the political and economic systems under their
nominal control, so their capital cannot concentrate the wealth to maintain large urban populations or the power to organize and control such
populations. The regal-ritual city is only a symbol of the state, not its
embodiment demographically. This is the case because the state is more
symbolic than actual, more dependent on the status of the ruler than on
inequalities of power and wealth.

URBAN IDEOLOGY

The spatial design of the regal-ritual city consists of palaces, castles,
mud forts, temples and ceremonial centers, and huts, all of which reflect
the organization of state society around kings, chiefs, or priestly rulers.
The architecture has highly ideological functions; it testifies to the city as
both a part of and apart from the rest of society—like it in that the
ideology that mandates the construction of the temples or palaces is
shared by all parts of the state, but different in that the regal-ritual
capital stands *primus inter pares* as the highest concentration of these
symbolic qualities. The village Rajput's mud hut is a poorer version of
the chief's fort; the local magnate's castle duplicates in a less refined way
the court of Charlemagne. The dispersed homestead of a Swazi commoner contains one section called the capital where the headman's
mother lives in a small-scale duplication of the ritual capital where the
chief's mother resides.

The ritual and symbolic edifices of the regal-ritual cities, their
nature, distribution, and shapes, are worked out differently according to
the ideology and cultural phraseology of a specific society. Thus, in
Southeast Asia, the regal-ritual city reflects the organization of the
heavens in its image. In Charlemagne's Aix-la-Chapelle, the spatial
distribution of the regal-ritual city depends on a combination of ritual
notions from Christianity merged with an attempted recreation of the
glory of a golden Rome.

Whatever the particular ideological components that define regal-
ritual ideology in each state society, the city remains the kingly or priestly
homestead writ large. Whether the homestead is defined by an image of
the divine or merely seen as a common household expanded and
glorified, the simple equation of the architecture of rule with the layout
of the regal-ritual settlement remains. Just as the segmentary states
contain few institutions of governance beyond the king or priest or
ruling clan, so their regal-ritual cities do not extend spatially into more

complex patterns than that derived from the household and household economy of the rulers.

In other segmentary state societies, specific cultural beliefs organize regal-ritual cities in unique fashions, even though the general outlines conform to the three societies discussed earlier. To provide a wider geographical illustration of the segmentary state and its attendant primary urban type, we will analyze two other examples very briefly.

Dahomey was a state society that arose in West Africa before the advent of European conquerors. Arensberg has described the capital of Dahomey as "simply one village among many in its form. It was one village, that of king and his royal sib and household, grown great." The housing compound of the typical Dahomean village became the royal capital; the village ancestral shrine became a royal one to be worshipped by the whole kingdom. The market found in all villages grew into the royal market. The many wives of the king became state officials, symbolic mothers linked by pseudo-kinship ties to all the subsidiary, dispersed magnates of the state. Other wives, the famous Amazons, formed the royal standing army. Arensberg sums up the quality of the regal-ritual center so clearly evident in Dahomey: "In every particular the city was a combination of the usual dispersed institutions of the countryside and like them in essential form. But in function it was a gathering of them into a single center, a node of ruling power."[9]

In traditional Southeast Asia, the court and capital of the ruler were an image of the supernatural world. Just as the king was perceived as a divine being, sometimes as a reincarnation of a particular god, so the architecture of the royal court was a replica on this earth of the heavenly world. The image of an ordered and ritualized existence, which the king's court represented, provided a model for the rest of the society.[10] State ceremonials and elaborate rituals were occasions on which the king in his regal-ritual capital personified the heavenly order and in consequence dramatized the ideal organization of the world for his followers. The spatial organization of the capital accentuated the importance of the four cardinal points of the Buddhist system. The king's palace stood at the center of both the state and ritual universe; subsidiary palaces surrounding his contained princes and court officials. How close these subsidiary palaces stood to the center indicated their relative status and the political and ritual preeminence of their occupants. The administrative organization of the state was also defined in large measure by cosmological criteria. In Burma the capital housed four chief ministers, each of whom had charge of a quarter of the capital and of the state.

[9]Arensberg, "The Urban in Cross-Cultural Perspective," p. 12.
[10]Heine-Geldern, "Conceptions of State and Kingship," pp. 17-18.

These chief ministers were conceived as earthly images of the four guardian dieties at the cardinal points. Four other officers were assigned supervision over one corner of the palace and capital. Each had a flag whose color corresponded to one particular side of Mount Meru, the mountain at the center of the universe in Buddhist belief. The principle of four or multiples of four continued through the official governmental structure, with four heralds, four royal messengers, and so forth.[11]

Just as the Swazi commoner homestead duplicates various features of the royal center (or vice versa; it is not important in which direction the transmission goes, for the ultimate goal is duplication), so the subsidiary courts in Southeast Asia emulated the capital. In traditional Thailand, individuals who originally owed their estates and positions to the king at times grew autonomous and became local magnates quite independent of royal control. Such magnates constructed their own courts and capitals. These subsidiary regal-ritual cities became "duplicates, on a smaller scale, [of] the same cosmologically oriented structure of government as that exhibited in all its grandeur by the royal capital."[12] A similar situation in Bali led to the proliferation of "exemplary centers," or regal-ritual settlements started by secondary and tertiary splinters from a presumed formerly unitary rulership. Each splinter tried to duplicate the original center of Gelgel, itself based on the glorified ancient empire of Majapahit.[13] In Bali as in Swaziland and Rajput India, this ideological duplication of an existent or mythological regal-ritual archetype links all settlements into a hierarchy based on ritual status and regal prestige.

The regal-ritual urban type occurs within the context of a particular type of state society, here called segmentary. The cultural role of such cities is predicated on their ideological function as ritual and prestige symbols for their residents. They are the elites of decentralized, relatively economically undifferentiated states. Shorn of this symbolic function, regal-ritual cities do not have the demographic base, nor do they perform the communication, transportation or productive functions often associated with cities. When ritual status and political prestige are considered, however, they obviously stand above merely rural settlements, although they remain linked to them by an ideological chain of emulation. This ideological chain forms a hierarchy of settlements from

[11]*Ibid.*, pp. 4-5.
[12]Riggs, *Thailand*, p. 82.
[13]Geertz, "Politics Past, Politics Present," pp. 5-6.

king's capital to rural village.[14] The ideological ties and continuity between regal-ritual cities and the larger society are not perpetuated in
other urban types where state power is stronger or urban economic
autonomy greater. The urban area becomes increasingly separated from
its rural hinterland as the power and wealth of state rulers increase.
Political exploitation and economic expropriation replace the common
ideology that binds the city to the society. Such is the case for the form of
the city discussed in the following chapter.

[14]The regal-ritual urban type may be significant for understanding what archaeologists have called cult centers in the formative periods of many early civilizations. Although
archaeologists usually consider such cult centers as not fully urban, their description of the
functions performed by such places accords well with the regal-ritual type presented here.
For a discussion of regal-ritual functions among the ancient Maya and the Khmers, see
Michael D. Coe, "Social Typology in the Tropical Forest Civilizations," *Comparative Studies
in Society and History*, IV, 1 (1961), and "A Model of Lowland Maya Community Structure,"
Southwestern Journal of Anthropology, XXI, 2 (1965), pp. 97-114. Paul Wheatley suggests that
the earliest cities in all pristine civilizations were of a form which could be labeled as
regal-ritual. See his *Pivot of the Four Quarters: A Preliminary Enquiry into the Origins and
Character of the Ancient Chinese City* (Chicago: Aldine, 1971).

4

Administrative
Cities

The systematic study of cities by social scientists has developed only in the last century and predominantly in the industrial nations of Western Europe and America. In part, the recent development of urban social science coincides with the general emergence of sociology and anthropology as scholarly fields. It also results, however, from the confrontation of modern industrial nations with the staggering urban problems that have grown up in the last hundred years. The overcrowding, ethnic conflicts, violence, disease, and personal anonymity found in contemporary industrial cities have called for explanation and analysis, whether in the journalistic and exposé style of American muckrakers and social critics, or the less impressionistic and presumably more objective view of sociologists. To be sure, archaeologists, historians, and architects studied cities in ancient and classical times or in other lands and cultures. Nevertheless, urban studies as a distinctive branch of social science most clearly develops alongside the social problems that have beset industrial cities over the last century.

It is perhaps no surprise then that early research on cities and the first theories to account for the urban world relied heavily on social conditions and spatial distribution found in cities of the contemporary Western world, especially American ones such as Chicago.[1] This limited

[1]See Francisco Benet, "Sociology Uncertain: The Ideology of the Rural-Urban Continuum," *Comparative Studies in Society and History*, VI, 1 (1963), p. 8.

view of cities meant that many qualities which perhaps only pertained to industrial or American cities were generalized to fit all urban places. In an influential article written in 1938, Louis Wirth, an American sociologist, identified secularism, heterogeneity, and anonymity as typical qualities of urban places.[2] Robert Redfield, one of the first American anthropologists to study the city, contrasted the small, isolated, family-oriented, and religious "folk society" with its nether image, secularized, impersonal, and cosmopolitan "urban society."[3] The same period saw Robert Burgess expound his concentric zone theory of urban growth and layout.[4] He postulated that various functional zones succeeded themselves in all cities. At the core came the central business district. This was surrounded by a zone of smaller retail establishments, slums and transient housing; and this in turn was succeeded by areas of working-class and upper-class residences, which gave way to a zone of suburban housing. Each zone, according to Burgess, had its own particular form of urban life, its own incidence of crime, divorce, commerce, alcoholism, and other social phenomena. Both the image of the urban world as propounded by Wirth and Redfield and the zonal theory of city space as advanced by Burgess rely almost exclusively on Western and industrial urban experience. The question remained: Would such notions apply as well to cities in other societies and nonindustrial nations as they did in Chicago and other American industrial metropolises?

Only in the last several decades has an alternative theory of the city emerged in American sociology. In 1955, Gideon Sjoberg suggested that then prevalent notions about cities and urban societies were too heavily dependent on the experience of industrial nations over the last century.[5] Instead of setting all cities into a common mold derived from the Chicago model, he divided the world's urban centers into two types, the preindustrial city and the industrial city. Sjoberg distinguished his two types on the basis of technological differences: Preindustrial cities were to be found in societies without sophisticated machine technology, where human and animal labor formed the basic productive system. Industrial cities predominated in the modernized nations of Western Europe and America where energy was derived from coal, petroleum, electricity, and atomic power. These energy sources completely altered man's control over his environment and the nature of his social institutions, including cities. Sjoberg suggested that many of the accepted notions about urbanism really applied only to industrial cities. For example, he

[2]Louis Wirth, "Urbanism as a Way of Life," *The American Journal of Sociology*, XLIV, 1 (1938).

[3]Redfield, "The Folk Society," *The American Journal of Sociology*, LII, 4 (1947).

[4]Robert E. Park, Ernest W. Burgess, and Roderick D. McKenzie, *The City* (Chicago: University of Chicago Press, 1925).

[5]Gideon Sjoberg, "The Preindustrial City," *The American Journal of Sociology*, LX, 5 (1955).

found that secularism, anonymity, central business districts, and loss of familial ties were not important diagnostics of his preindustrial urban type. These were urban qualities that pertained mainly to the industrial form of the city.

The concept of the preindustrial city has removed much of the ethnocentrism and limited historical perspective found in urban sociology and anthropology. But there are pitfalls in this approach that must be recognized and rectified before a better understanding of cities in nonindustrial societies can be achieved. The greatest difficulty with Sjoberg's thesis is his belief that *all* preindustrial cities fall into a single type. The result is a highly stylized portrait of cities in the past with a historical perspective "as flat as a pancake and vacant as a prairie."[6] In Sjoberg's scheme, some regal-ritual cities discussed in the previous chapter would be considered nonindustrial cities and others would not (depending on whether or not the society was literate). They would all be merged into a common category including ancient cities of the Near East, classical cities of the Mediterranean, medieval cities of Europe, and contemporary cities of the underdeveloped nations such as Afghanistan, Korea, and India. By squeezing what might more meaningfully be seen as many different types of cities into a single category—preindustrial—Sjoberg misses the diversity of human urban experience and overlooks different patterns of relationship between city and state society.

Three types of nonindustrial cities are distinguished in this book for the period before the advent of industrialism, only one of which fits Sjoberg's conception of the preindustrial city. The objective of this chapter is to discuss the administrative city, a form of urbanism that conforms to Sjoberg's preindustrial model. The previous chapter analyzed the regal-ritual city, a preindustrial urban type that Sjoberg would not recognize as such. The succeeding chapter describes the mercantile city, a form of urbanism that preexisted industrial societies but that does not fit well with Sjoberg's thesis.

According to Sjoberg, two essential traits link the preindustrial city to the larger state society. The first of these concerns the origins and spread of preindustrial cities. Rather than arising because of a favorable location for commerce or transportation, rather than having an economic foundation, preindustrial cities grow up, in the Sjoberg thesis, as centers of administration for the state society.[7] They are established by emperors, kings, and princes as nodal points from which to control the population and territory of their domains. Cities centralize the official

⁶Sylvia Thrupp, "The Creativity of Cities: A Review Article," *Comparative Studies in Society and History*, IV, 1 (1961).

⁷Sjoberg, *The Preindustrial City, Past and Present* (New York: The Free Press, 1960), pp. 68-69.

apparatus, the transportation links, and the economic power needed to control and rule a state society. In this sense, all preindustrial cities are capitals. Urban places spread over the countryside as the dominion of emperors, kings, or princes spreads. They serve as market and trade centers for goods; but such economic functions are secondary and exist only because of the protection afforded them by the ruling power. As a corollary to the idea of the preindustrial city as capital of the state, Sjoberg believes that all preindustrial state rulers lived in urban places. Just as the city controls the state, so the ruling elite controls the city and represents the premier class in a rigid urban social hierarchy.

The material presented in the preceding chapter on regal-ritual cities indicates that not all urban places were repositories of the power and political control that Sjoberg deems typical of preindustrial cities. Indeed, the ritual preeminence of such cities highlighted how little real power and social control was exercised by titular state leaders, and how much was dispersed through every corner of the segmentary state society. In the succeeding chapter we will see that under certain economic conditions and political situations, preindustrial urban locales are not capitals of state power, are not residences of the state rulers, and are relatively free of state control. Yet some cities before the advent of industrialism did fit the preindustrial urban model advanced by Sjoberg. This chapter portrays the internal organization and external adaptation of this type of city, here called "administrative" to indicate its origins at the behest of the ruling elite and its functions as an organ of state government.

In what ways, then, does the administrative urban type differ from the regal-ritual type discussed in the previous chapter? There is a strong but superficial appearance of continuity. The administrative city, like the regal-ritual city, is the residence of the state elite and a center of prestige and ritual functions. The political and ritual edifices of the state society—palaces, temples, walls, mausoleums—define to a major extent the urban ideology of the administrative city. However, administrative settlements are urban not only in ideological functions but also in organization. Their populations are large, densely settled, heterogeneous in occupation, and often ethnically varied. The existence of this stable population base is the factor intrinsic to the administrative city that differentiates it from the regal-ritual urban type. Besides being a population center, administrative cities contain and perform many more functions of communication and transportation. They centralize commerce, crafts, and other occupational specialities. Urban organization thus becomes an increasingly significant factor in the separation of the city from its surrounding rural area. The city is not only a citadel or ceremonial settlement. It is a node of political, economic, and communicative links with the surrounding countryside. As occupational specialization and increased resident population grow to characterize the city, so, too, does an urban class structure appear. This urban class structure is dependent on different sources of power and different amounts of wealth enjoyed by urban residents. The poor of the city appear and play a large, if often negative and violent, role in the urban settlement. Increasing differentiation in power, wealth, and position within the administrative city means that various institutions develop to organize the city populace or to maintain political and economic order within it. Such institutions are peculiar to urban areas. Municipal government, citizen status, guild associations, and ward allegiances organize the city populace and hinder the discontent and potential for rebellion ever present in such administrative urban places.

With a specifically urban population and a distinctly urban pattern of social organization, the administrative city is further from the rural countryside in ideology and life-style than the regal-ritual type is. The patterns of belief and social life, the cultural "rules" of the state society, may remain basically the same in village and city. The urban area, on the other hand, concentrates a sophistication—an elaborateness of custom and ideology—that mark it off sharply from the rural zone. Rather than a hiatus in belief, rather than an antagonism based on wholly different urban and rural patterns, the administrative city is simply so much more than its rural environs that rural areas appear culturally denuded, socially deficient, and ideologically backward by comparison. The city may still reflect the countryside, but it does so with such intensity that it appears to have its own independent luminosity.

BUREAUCRATIC STATE
AND ADMINISTRATIVE CITY

What conditions in the wider society lie behind the existence of cities that conform to the administrative urban type? According to the typology of primary urbanism, administrative cities are associated with bureaucratic (strong) state power and externally dependent urban economy, both of which give preeminence to administrative cultural roles in the city. The heightened power and wealth of the state mandate the demographic growth of the city, the development of urban commercial and communication facilities, and the existence of widely separated urban social classes. The city thus becomes a repository of state strength and riches but not a primary source of them. The source of food for the city and its rulers, and therefore the source of wealth and power in the state, is the peasant producers in the rural areas. This dependency determines the interactional ties linking administrative cities with the larger society. Whereas the riches of regal-ritual cities lay in their treasured ritual or symbolic kingship, the wealth of administrative cities lies in the grain requisitioned by the ruling elite and consumed or converted into gold, silver, and luxury goods in their urban settlements. The administrative city is a locus of wealth extracted from the agricultural countryside. It is a place of temples and palaces, of splendor and luxury in which the state rulers dissipate and display their wealth won elsewhere. The city becomes a node of the power and administration that maintain the ruling elite's control over the rural food source. It becomes a market in which to convert wheat, rice, and maize into swords, servants, gold, and silk. Even when the city does produce wealth autonomously—through large-scale and long-distance trade—this source of riches is rigorously controlled through law and taxation so as to serve the ruling elite. Commerce in the city is subjected to the same state administrative control as rules the rural areas; and merchant wealth, like peasant produce, is either suppressed as a threat to political stability or extracted to subsidize the state. Consumption of rural capital and control of merchant wealth are the major activities of the state and form the adaptive pattern of administrative cities. These points are more fully illustrated in the case material that follows.

The state societies discussed in this chapter are therefore highly cohesive and centralized polities. No longer segmentary or mainly symbolic, they depend on great concentrations of power by a ruling elite and a well-developed class system based on wealth and political inequalities among individuals. Since the economic base on which such state societies depends is peasant subsistence agriculture (that is, cultivation of food staples rather than market-destined crops), the state's power is most evident in the ability to extract a large measure of the peasants' productivity. The effectiveness of state government and the enrichment of its ruling elite directly relate to how efficiently the state can administer peasant agriculture for its own purposes.

As the interactional (and exploitative) links between coercive state and oppressed peasant grow stronger, the state becomes more powerful and more separated from the rural countryside. Connected by political and economic necessity to the peasant producer, the powerful state elite nevertheless accentuates ideological and social distinctions that remove them—as a highly privileged group—from the larger society. No longer are the king and courtier, sultan and emir, or shogun and daimyo merely most prestigious in a status hierarchy that subsumes the majority of the population (as in the Rajput and Swazi segmentary states). The elite are qualitatively separate from the rural peasantry. No peasant can hope to duplicate the elite life-style—not because as in Swaziland the chief concentrates most prestige or because as in Southeast Asia the king embodies the divine—but because the peasant cannot duplicate the economic wherewithal, military might, and political power of a shogun, king, or sultan. Although the elite is still surrounded with prestige, still accorded divine status or inspiration, the ideological aspects of rule serve mainly as the velvet glove that softens the iron hand of state power. As state centralization increases, the ideology and the life-style of the elite move further and further from peasant life. They become a sophisticated, elaborate, and highly codified world view enjoyed by the ruler and scarcely grasped by the rural peasantry.

Alteration in the organization of the ruling elite is reflected in its increased power and economic resources in comparison with segmentary states. The office of the supreme ruler—king or shogun—may still be filled by ascription, but the power and autonomy of the lower hereditary elite are greatly curtailed. A centralized bureaucratic system emerges as the primary method of state administration, although the state societies to be discussed in this chapter exhibit substantial variation in how successfully it is instituted. The Mamluk regime depended on new military cadres gaining prominence in each generation; state offices therefore never became the hereditary possessions of elite families. Emirs and Mamluks earned salaries from the state and had little control over the peasant lands that produced their income. Similar developments occurred in seventeenth-century France, although political centralization took a somewhat different course there because of the power of feudal elements. French kings increasingly converted formerly autonomous feudal lords into subservient courtiers. They drafted wealthy merchants into state government and ennobled them so as to dilute the hereditary elite. The Tokugawa shogun required warrior lords to live in his castle town and increasingly alienated them from their local power bases. The warrior lords became "feudal" hostages of an emerging bureaucratic system in the capital, where the sumptuous extravagance that validated their elite status also impoverished them and bound them even more tightly to the dictates of the central ruler. In all these cases, state functions are performed by appointees of the king, shogun, or sultan. The positions of such appointees depend on personal qualifications and royal favor rather than on hereditary status. Just as the peasant is made subservient to the powerful state, so the subsidiary elite who might threaten the ruler's position are made servants of the Crown.

Stripped in varying degrees of their personal followings, their economic self-sufficiency, and their provincial autonomy, such men act as agents of central power rather than as small-scale duplicates of it (as held true in segmentary states).

No longer held together by prestige, kin hierarchies, or ideological emulation alone, the state administers on a territorial basis. Political subordinates are linked to the central government by chains of command, bureaus, and a hierarchy of official positions. The resulting state, at its strongest, is able to coalesce politically large regions. It does so effectively in terms of extracting the peasants' productivity and suppressing peasant rebellion and elite revolt. The term "bureaucratic state," which we shall adopt for such polities, emphasizes a changed basis of administration and a new order of centralization, political cohesiveness, and economic direction. These are exhibited by the state societies of seventeenth-century France, the Mamluk Near East, Tokugawa Japan and many other preindustrial political systems.

The Mamluk Empire

From the time of Muhammad and the advent of Islam in the Near East, dynasties and their administrative cities formed, governed, and then decayed. A detailed portrait exists of the city under the Mamluk Empire (1260–1517).[8] During its period of ascendancy, Mamluk state society represented a highly centralized polity with government based on territorial and bureaucratic principles. The Mamluks formed the ruling elite, military forces, and premier urban residents in the state. They were recruited in their youth from the Caucasus region and the Russian steppes, and were attached as slaves to the households of currently ruling Mamluks. Because the children of Mamluks were not permitted to inherit the political offices of their fathers, each generation saw a new set of slaves brought down from the North. These slaves

[8]The following materials on the Mamluk state and its administrative cities are derived from Ira M. Lapidus, "Muslim Cities and Islamic Societies" in *Middle Eastern Cities: A Symposium on Ancient, Islamic, and Contemporary Middle Eastern Urbanism*, Ira M. Lapidus, ed. (Berkeley: University of California Press, 1969); Ira M. Lapidus, *Muslim Cities in the Later Middle Ages* (Cambridge, Massachusetts: Harvard University Press, 1967); Ira M. Lapidus, "Muslim Urban Society in Mamluk Syria," in *Papers on Islamic History: I. The Islamic City: A Colloquium*, A.H. Hourani and S.M. Stern, eds. (Oxford: Bruno Cassirer Ltd., 1970); A.H. Hourani, "Introduction: The Islamic City in the Light of Recent Research," in *Papers on Islamic History: I. The Islamic City: A Colloquium*, A.H. Hourani and S.M. Stern, eds. (Oxford: Bruno Cassirer Ltd., 1970); G.E. Von Grunebaum, *Islam: Essays in the Nature and Growth of a Cultural Tradition*, Memoirs of the American Anthropological Association, Memoir #81, *The American Anthropologist*, LVII, 2, Part 2 (1955).

would eventually become the highest state officials and military commanders. Apart from the Mamluk military elite that controlled the state, an elaborate bureaucracy of scribes, court officials, revenue collectors, and legal advisors existed. This bureaucracy was drawn from the non-Mamluk population.

Cairo was the major seat of Mamluk power, the residence of the sultan or ruler of the state, the location of the central bureaucracy and army, and the administrative focus of an empire that stretched from contemporary Egypt into Syria and Turkey. Other major administrative cities were Aleppo and Damascus, each of whose populations exceeded fifty thousand. Just as Cairo was governed by the sultan, so other Mamluk cities were administered through governors appointed by the sultan and drawn from the emirs, a class that constituted the high ranking Mamluks resident in an urban settlement. Every Mamluk emir had many lower ranking Mamluks who were attached to his urban household as slaves and who formed a personal military force. These Mamluk households formed the major focuses of wealth and political power in the cities. They were also the major instruments of state administration and exploitation of the indigenous populace.

The wealth and power of the Mamluk emirs and their households emerged from their domination of the countryside and their taxation of the peasants' productivity. Each Mamluk officer received a state salary (fixed by rank) that came to him partially in coin and partially in kind. Salaries were mainly paid from land revenue (derived from taxation of peasants) expressly set aside for support of state military and administrative officers. The Mamluk administrative and military elite played a major role not only in urban political order, but also in the commercial orientation and religious organization of the city. Because the Mamluk emirs were richer than any other segment of society, and because their military retainers and official staff were so numerous, their household economy greatly influenced the city's commerce. An emir might earn annually as much as two thousand workers, and emirs' urban residences were storehouses of precious metals, jewels, weapons, grain, and other luxury and subsistence goods. High ranking Mamluks were therefore the largest consumers of artisan skills and luxury commercial commodities in the city. Mamluks also controlled a major source of the urban food supply. In order to convert into money that part of their salaries paid to them in grain, Mamluks speculated in the grain market. They in large measure determined the supply and price of this basic foodstuff for the nonagricultural urban populace. Emirs could also influence the organization of the urban market place and the distribution of crafts, as for example when they obtained from the sultan the right to build markets and to move certain artisans into them. Not only in political organization, therefore, but also in basic food supply and market disposition, the city was administered by the Mamluk ruling elite.

French Absolutism

By the early sixteenth century, a developing centralized monarchy had begun to fashion a French nation out of the decentralized medieval polity of fiefs and feudatories, a nation based on a bureaucratic state similar to the Mamluks'.[9] The feudal nobility continued to possess titles, wealth, and influence. However, the military preeminence of the French kings, their territorial possessions (expanded by marriage and conquest), their royal justice and royal coinage, had greatly limited the sovereignty of the hereditary elite. The power of the French kings similarly encroached upon and restricted the autonomy of popular assemblies such as the Estates and the Parlement (court of justice). Provincial governors, drawn from the highest nobility and often in the past semi-independent, were increasingly supervised by royal bureaucrats (*intendants*) periodically sent out on inspection tours by the king. This intendant system later developed into the permanent administrative pattern for the provinces of France. Intendants and other state administrators were increasingly drawn from among the wealthy merchants of Paris and other cities and appointed directly by the king. Rather than by a total alteration in the state society, "the centralized bureaucratic state developed *within* the loose federation of petty sovereignties based on immemorial custom. It was not a revolution, but a dissolving picture."[10]

Yet state centralization and royal power did not develop at a steady and inexorable pace. Various periods saw royal authority reduced or even shattered and witnessed a resurgence of both provincial and urban autonomy. Such a decline in state centralization occurred in the sixteenth century during the period of religious antagonism between French Catholics and Protestants. The next imposition of royal authority, under the Bourbon kings of the seventeenth and eighteenth centuries—which we view later in this chapter from the vantage of Paris—led to reconstitution of French royal power and state centralization to a degree hitherto unknown.

[9]Albert Guerard discusses the formation of a strong French state during this period in *The Life and Death of an Ideal: France in the Classical Age* (New York: Charles Scribner's Sons, 1928). The following material on Paris is taken from Orest Ranum, *Paris in the Age of Absolutism: An Essay* (New York: John Wiley & Sons, Inc., 1968).
[10]Guerard, *The Life and Death of an Ideal*, p. 164.

Tokugawa Centralized Feudalism

Tokugawa Japan (1600–1858) witnessed one of the most rapid and large-scale periods of urban growth known in the preindustrial world. By 1700, Edo, the premier city in Japan, numbered nearly one million inhabitants. At the same time, Osaka and Kyoto each contained about three hundred thousand people, and ten percent of the Japanese population lived in cities of over ten thousand.[11] Massive urbanization in Japan developed from 1580 to 1610 when the many dispersed market towns, shrine centers, and military fortresses were displaced by centrally located cities. These coalesced around the castles of the Tokugawa military elite and their political dependents. Such cities dominated the countryside and acted as centers of power, commerce, and sophistication. The state ruling elite maintained their residence and military garrisons in such "castle towns," and administered the city, its commerce and merchants, and its political life and class divisions just as they ruled the peasant cultivators of the rural countryside.

The growth of large castle towns in Japan evolved from a general political centralization and pacification late in the sixteenth century. The *shogun*, drawn from the Tokugawa family, stood atop the power pyramid and directly administered one-quarter of the country. The shogun's capital was Edo (later known as Tokyo), but his authority also extended to other cities, such as commercial Osaka and Kyoto. The shogun maintained a large court of *samurai*, or warriors, for the military protection and bureaucratic administration of his hereditary possessions. Ranking below the shogun were approximately 260 "feudal lords" called *daimyo*, some of whom owed allegiance, military service, and revenue payments to the shogun, and others of whom were not so bound. Every daimyo also had a hereditary domain and a personal following of warriors to protect and administer his possessions. Although daimyos were permitted relative autonomy within their domains, the power of the shogun and the central warrior bureaucracy were continually impressed upon them. All daimyos were required to spend every other year in residence at the capital in Edo; their wives and heirs were forced to be permanent

[11]Takeo Yazaki, *Social Change and the City in Japan: From Earliest Times Through the Industrial Revolution*, trans. by David L. Swain (Japan Publications, Inc., 1968), p. 134; other sources of information on Tokugawa Japan and its castle towns are Charles David Sheldon, *The Rise of the Merchant Class in Tokugawa Japan, 1600–1868. An Introductory Survey* (Locust Valley, New York: Published for the Association of Asian Studies by J.J. Augustin Incorporated, 1958), and John Whitney Hall, "The Castle Town and Japan's Modern Urbanization," *The Far Eastern Quarterly*, XV, 1 (1955).

hostages in attendance at the shogun's court. Enforced residence in Edo not only kept the daimyos under constant central supervision; it also promoted great population and wealth concentration in the capital. To the extent that the daimyos expended great sums of wealth in maintaining their Edo residences (a requirement for their continued prestige), they impoverished their home localities and expended in luxurious display funds that might have served to foment rebellion from the central government.

Political development throughout Tokugawa times favored the rule of the shogun over the daimyos, and saw the centralization of the economy and population in the shogun's capital city. This period also witnessed the transformation of the samurai from a warrior class pledging personal allegiance to daimyo or shogun into salaried bureaucrats whose positions almost exclusively depended on appointment and favor by the central ruler or his great dependents. "Centralized feudalism" is the label that has been applied to the Tokugawa regime. Such a term emphasizes the combination of strong central authority with an ideology of political relations based on paternalism and personal ties. [12]

URBAN ADAPTATION

The administrative city is a political extension of the bureaucratic state. It serves as the residence of the state elite and the political center from which the elite rules the countryside. The city functions as the nodal point of the bureaucratic state and integrates the economic, military, and political administration of the peasant countryside. A source of neither wealth nor political power in its own right, the city is a receptacle of commodities and a repository of domination derived by the state from a subservient rural populace. For just as the elite is predatory, so too is the administrative city. Its population, occupational specialization, and architecture are constructed from the rice paddies of the Japanese cultivator or the wheat fields of the French peasant. The city's links to the larger society are economic and political ones that permit the conversion of the countryside's resources into urban subsistence and luxury. These interactional ties between city and hinterland are patterned through the state. Thus adaptation of administrative city to the larger society becomes equivalent to the organization of coercive force and wealth inequalities embodied in the bureaucratic state. Those who exer-

[12]Hall, "The Castle Town and Japan's Modern Urbanization," p. 73.

cise empire over the rural peasant control the administrative city because the city cannot exist in a power vacuum that cuts its interactional ties with the surrounding region.

Since the administrative city is only a bastion of state power and not a source of state power, the urban locale plays a generally passive role in state upheavals, even though its existence and prosperity depend on the stability of the state regime. There are mass protests and even outright rebellions by the city populace. However, their chances for success or even amelioration of harsh conditions ultimately rest on factional struggle within the ruling elite itself or the presence of an external conquering power that threatens the state. Palace revolts and dynastic upheavals through conquest are the major avenues by which the city's condition is altered (whether for better or worse). Factional rearrangement of the state rulers or their replacement by another state elite is necessarily echoed in the city's condition. But rarely if ever is the city the source of change or the starting point of power and wealth in the new regime.

Similarly, the growth of administrative urban centers is an adjunct of state power. For administrative as well as prestige reasons, the conquering king, shogun, or sultan endows cities along the path of his conquests and in the wake of his territorial aggrandizement. Such city endowments may on occasion prove profitless because of poor location; in other situations, the kingly site may coincide with economic nodality or military security and thus prosper and grow. But the initiative for city formation and the spread of urbanization rest with state power. Indeed, very often the commercial nodality of such city endowments develops precisely because of the state definition of the area as central and strategic (as in Tokugawa Japan). A ruler decides for administrative reasons, for military protection, or merely from whim to move his capital city to another site; and with a great upheaval of courtiers, bureaucrats, merchants, artisans, and laborers, the administrative city is resurrected in another place. Urbanization, therefore, is derivative not of communication function, commercial nodality, or surrounding agricultural fertility, but rather of the dictates and power of the bureaucratic state. The state may or may not consider any of these factors in its disposition of state administration and its subsidy of urban growth.

The urban hierarchy that develops in bureaucratic state societies does not rest on a chain of ideological emulation linking the premier regal-ritual city with secondary ones. Neither does it depend on a gradation of communication, transportation, and commercial services that rank local, regional, and national urban places into an industrial pattern of urban dominance. Administrative cities are linked into an urban hierarchy based on their position in state administration, their relative importance in the performance of bureaucratic functions, and the relative size and strength of their military and civil establishments representing the state. The relationship among capital, provincial, and local administrative centers is therefore a political one.

This pattern of administrative hierarchy is modified in two ways that determine a range of secondary variation in the urbanism of the bureaucratic state type. These variations develop from particular historical circumstances that may be present in some bureaucratic state societies and absent in others. One variant consists of the persistence of decentralized power holders, such as a feudal elite, in what were formerly regal-ritual cities. Such cities may not be incorporated as administrative places in the encroaching bureaucratic state. Their survival means that an atrophied urban hierarchy of prestige and ideological emulation may persist alongside the administrative one. Seventeenth-century France perhaps provides the best example of this variant among the cases given in this chapter. However, the persistence of the feudal lords in their regal-ritual castles (like those of Charlemagne and his magnates) was already minimal and underwent an even further deterioration as the French bureaucratic state grew more powerful.

The other variant of the administrative urban hierarchy emerges as a pattern complementary to the bureaucratic state, rather than merely an atavism of former times. The occupational specialization and and heterogeneity *within* administrative cities (see urban organization later in this chapter) has its analogue in the relations *between* cities. Some urban places in bureaucratic state societies are specialized commercial emporiums or ritual sanctuaries. Osaka in Tokugawa Japan, Marseilles in seventeenth-century France, Shanghai in traditional China, Banaras in pre-British India, and Mecca in the Muslim Near East represent such specialized commercial or ritual urban settlements. Their special positions may originate under conditions long antecedent to the bureaucratic state in which they are incorporated at any particular moment. Their persistence may rely more heavily on trade and ritual functions (as opposed to political power) than those cities that are simply state administrative creations. But just as urban merchants and religious notables within a city operate in contexts different from but not independent of the state elite, so the functional specialization of commercial and ritual cities shows a similar pattern. Such specialization does not give rise to a separate pattern of urban political relations with the state. Nor does it encourage an urbanism where wealth and prestige are less at the state's service. Although their existence is not mainly predicated on their administrative functions and they therefore stand apart from the urban administrative hierarchy, such cities are as much administered by the state as those urban places that primarily house bureaucrats, soldiers, and other state functionaries. So long as the bureaucratic state remains strong, such cities are subordinated to the administrative hierarchy of urban places. Their commercial wealth or ritual sanctity becomes an adjunct of the state's power or prestige.

A predominantly administrative urban hierarchy means that when the ruling dynasty or government is shattered, or when the state decides for administrative convenience to shift its disposition of official duties, urban places may rise and fall in importance. Their relations with other cities in the hierarchy may undergo significant change. Conservation of facilities and funds or strategic military position and existent fortifications may lead one dynasty or government to remain in the administrative settlements of its predecessors. The important point is that such decisions lie outside the city and rest with state ruling powers. The functions of administrative cities as well, therefore, as their positions in an urban hierarchy are derivative, not self-generated.

Mamluk cities, seventeenth-century Paris, and Tokugawa castle towns clearly illustrate the preponderance of administrative cultural roles (lodged with the state elite) in the external adaptation of cities set in bureaucratic states.

Mamluk Cities

In Mamluk cities, the organization of urban government, the maintenance of urban amenities, the punishment of urban legal and moral derelicts, and the provision of urban food supply all depended on the activities of the Mamluk elite and its involvement in urban affairs. Merchants, artisans, lower classes, and the criminal underworld appeared in Mamluk cities, and urban locales developed cohesive communal quarters and influential men apart from the ruling elite. Nevertheless, such cities existed primarily as administrative centers for highly centralized states and formed residences for the ruling elite of such states. Whenever through great wealth and a sense of religious obligation or noblesse oblige, a Mamluk governor repaired roads, built fortifications, or endowed mosques and schools, the city's sophistication grew and its facilities increased. Whenever through anarchy in the state, decreasing land revenues, or personal disposition, Mamluk governors let city walls fall into decay, mosques deteriorate, markets go unbuilt, and streets go unrepaired, urban facilities declined and the city became less sophisticated and of less renown.

Maintenance of city facilities depended not only on Mamluk wealth; it also depended on the fact that Mamluk governors were the only elements in the urban population who could effectively organize labor and raw materials on a large scale. The Mamluk elite extracted corvée labor from the city populace, especially for the rebuilding of the city's protective walls. The Mamluk state also controlled building materials such as wood and quarried stone, and therefore greatly influenced the nature of urban construction and its costs. Organization and materials, power and efficiency emanated from the state, not from within the city.

At the nucleus of the city, the citadel or fort and the governor's palace protected the urban locale and served as the bastion of Mamluk power. The residences of other leading emirs and Mamluks were clustered in this area. Central business districts existed where long rows of shops, mosques, and schools formed the commercial and social focus of the city. Apart from the citadel and the central markets, the city was divided into numerous ethnically, religiously, and commercially separate quarters that acted like islands of communal life and allegiance within the city. Damascus had about seventy and Aleppo contained over fifty of these relatively close knit and homogeneous quarters, each of which contained on the average some one thousand people or fewer. Each quarter was a distinctive social realm with residences, a local market, mosques, and a great door that could be closed to seal off the quarter from the outside. The cohesion of some quarters depended on religion or sect: Jews, Christians, and different Muslim sects each had separate quarters in the city. Other quarters cohered around differences in ethnicity, craft specialization, and village of origin. Ascriptive and occupational criteria, rather than economic class, determined the distribution and organization of the urban population.

The Mamluk state recognized and controlled the majority of the urban populace through their quarter membership, rather than as individuals. The Mamluk governor selected a chief for each quarter from among the notables resident in it. The state set taxes on the quarter as a corporate unit, and the quarter chief's role was to apportion and collect this levy from his constituents. The state also placed a corporate responsibility on the quarter for the apprehension of criminals and the payment of blood money (when a quarter resident wounded or killed someone in another quarter).

As a parallel to the state's corporate treatment of the quarter and perhaps as a product of that treatment, the strongest community identification in Mamluk cities existed within a quarter. The quarter was the highest level of allegiance for the lower urban classes—an allegiance reinforced by ethnicity, religion, kinship, and village origins. Identification with a quarter led the individual to view other quarters with hostility, and thus prevented an allegiance to the city at large. Quarter membership was also the basis for the formation of the strongest urban associations found in Mamluk cities. Guilds and ·occupational associations, to the extent that they existed in spite of religious opposition, were weak creatures of the state ruling elite. However, gangs of young men, often of recent village origin and usually located in quarters outside the city walls, represented the only associations within the Mamluk city that sporadically threatened the monopoly of power enjoyed by the Mamluk elite. Such gangs had distinctive hair styles and robes and were under the control of the chief of the particular quarter. They served as defenders of their quarters against other urban residents, as assassins of oppressive state officials, and as leaders of the resistance against excessive taxation. Yet their role was not solely beneficial, for such gangs also often organized theft and protection rackets in the city and made prey of their fellow urbanites rather than the Mamluk rulers. In a strange but politically expedient form of co-optation, the Mamluks sometimes enlisted these gangs as paramilitary auxiliaries, a practice analogous to the (random but disproportionate) drafting of the ghetto poor into the United States Army during the Vietnam war.

Other than the organization of quarters, no formal municipal government existed in Mamluk cities. However, non-Mamluk urban notables acted as informal intermediaries between the state rulers and the majority of the urban populace. Although beneath the Mamluk elite in wealth, prestige, and most importantly, power, they performed important mercantile, ideological, and administrative functions that linked state rule and revenue with the city's internal social order and economy.

Those urban notables who were religious leaders, or *ulama,* acted as judges, prayer leaders, scholars, Koranic readers, and mosque officials. Because their religious learning was respected by all social classes, these men not only provided ideological leadership to the city, but also supervised many social and legal activities, such as marriage, divorce, guardianship, wills, inheritances, religious endowments, property transfers, and commercial transactions. They also performed urban administrative roles for the state by acting as market inspectors and mosque officers. Unlike Mamluk status, which could only be gained by birth, the prestigious and influential position of the religious leader was attained by many people. This achieved status included men appointed by the state, sons of Mamluks, merchants, craftsmen, and manual workers.

The role of the religious notables was to mediate the dictates of the Mamluk state rulers with the requirements of the urban population. Their goals were to maintain a stable social condition within the city and to pursue a social order consistent with Islamic religion. They were used by the state to articulate its decrees in a popular fashion—for instance, to curtail popular urban opposition to new or increased taxation, or to demonstrate against craft associations—but they often appealed to the state against excessive exploitation of the urban populace or for subsidy of public works and religious institutions. Although they tried to suppress discontent in the city, religious leaders were also in the forefront of the popular rebellions that arose when state exactions became extremely oppressive or when the Mamluk social order was in a period of weakness. The religious notables represented a subsidiary locus of authority within the city, an authority infinitely weaker than Mamluk control because it depended on respect for religious learning rather than on physical force.

In times of interregnum when state political power was at an ebb, the role of the religious notables as a stabilizing factor was at its greatest. Such periods of anarchy evoked violence and economic disruption within the city. Under such conditions, the religious leaders would support conquerors, a new regime, or any other political authority that promised to suppress internal dissension and reinstate a pacific Islamic social order. The religious leaders were loyal to the city, not to a particular ruling elite. However, they were powerless to effect social control without the external agency of state power and a ruling elite that also controlled the peasant countryside.

Merchant notables played an intermediary role in commerce similar to that of the religious leaders in civic affairs. Although merchants were often extremely wealthy and owned large amounts of urban property, their commerce was heavily dependent on the Mamluk elite. Merchants and mercantile wealth therefore never developed to any degree as an alternative source of power within the state. Commerce revolved about the Mamluks as suppliers of grain and consumers of luxury goods. Merchants converted grain into gold and silver, and they also acted as financial agents or state bankers for the Mamluk regime. Long distance trade depended on good political relations established by the state; it also required the state to insure the safety of caravan routes often threatened by pastoral nomads. Because the ultimate guarantee for wealth was political power, the merchants' riches were continually threatened with confiscation by the Mamluk elite. Loans given Mamluk rulers by merchants often were not repaid; forced purchases of goods at highly inflated rates were often required of merchants by their Mamluk overlords; and repressive taxation was an ever present threat to the merchants' capital.

The largest part of the city population consisted of neither Mamluk elite nor urban notable, but commoners such as shopkeepers, craftsmen, peddlers, and manual workers; disreputables such as slave dealers, butchers, dog handlers, wrestlers, and funeral workers; and such outcasts as thieves, gamblers, and prostitutes.

Parisian Civic Decline

Paris at the end of the sixteenth century was both a leading commercial center and the residence of the king of France. The city's commercial prominence meant that many urban dwellers grew rich in trade, and that Parisian economic life centered in guild associations of wholesalers, retailers, and artisans. The political importance of Paris rested on the presence of the French king and his court as the premier urban residents. The king "possessed the largest, strongest, and finest palaces and chateaus, received more guests, held a finer court, had more prayers said for him, and bought more than anyone else in the city."[13] The king (and his court) not only stimulated the commercial growth of the city through consumption of luxury goods and financing of urban construction. He also served as the military protector of the city and its merchants.

Paris never enjoyed the extensive municipal liberties that were granted other European cities of the Middle Ages (to be discussed in the next chapter). The city was always directly administered by the king of France. However, the king's power in urban affairs was limited, both because a wealthy merchant class exercised considerable autonomy in civic government and also because guild associations legislated many aspects of urban economic and social life. Yet like Mamluk cities, popular allegiance to Paris apart from its wealth and state functions was limited by the highly compartmentalized and hierarchical nature of Parisian social life. Clergy, wholesale merchants, retail traders, artisans, and royal officials each lived in virtually separate social domains within the urban sphere—with different leaders, status levels, wealth sources, and ideologies. The very strength of such formal and informal associations, whether guild, noble, or religious, and the hereditary or economic distinctions that separated noble from commoner or wholesaler from craftsman discouraged cohesion in the city.

Yet the possibilities for enrichment from large-scale commerce and the French king's need for money and support against his feudal nobles did not permit a complete isolation of the social divisions within the city. Large merchants grew wealthy and politically influential, especially in the religious wars of the latter sixteenth century and during a time of

[13]Ranum, *Paris in the Age of Absolutism*, p. 5.

decreasing state potency under the last Valois rulers. These urban merchant notables provided the basis for a degree of Parisian civic autonomy from state administration in the sixteenth century and temporarily in the seventeenth. But as royal power increased and solidified after the sixteenth-century religious wars; as the hereditary aristocracy lost its traditional sovereignty; as the merchant notables themselves replaced a bourgeois identification with a noble one; and as they gained royal offices through purchase from a king attempting to augment his royal purse, such merchants became part of the state bureaucratic machinery. In turn, the direction of the city passed increasingly into the hands of kings determined to remove any threat to the royal power that might remain in the urban sphere.

Parisian autonomy at the close of the sixteenth century rested in the elected officials of the *bureau de ville*. Control over the five positions in the bureau de ville and over leadership in each of the urban wards fell to some two hundred Parisian families that formed an oligarchy of property holders and leading merchants. The bureau de ville regulated urban trade, levied city taxes, maintained urban defenses and magistrates, and provided street cleaning and drinking water for the urban populace. The leading wholesalers and property owners who operated the municipal government were also royal judges, sat on royal councils, and influenced provincial politics because they generally owned country estates. Although these urban notables were called "bourgeois," they formed a nearly hereditary urban elite that desired to differentiate itself in prestige and social position from the less wealthy and less influential retailers and artisans.

Civic autonomy also emerged from the economic and social self-regulation practiced by the craft and trade guilds. The ritual and fraternal ties that bound guildsmen together formed the basis for concerted action and communal spirit outside the direct administration of the state. Thus, merchant notables and guild associations taken together meant that much of the economic, political, and social life of Paris was controlled by urban residents who stood apart from the nobility and from royal power.

Yet even before the sixteenth century, the kings of France heavily intruded into municipal affairs. A governor of Paris, appointed by the king, supervised the bureau de ville's proceedings. This situation generated many quarrels over authority and much confusion of powers. The king commonly intervened in municipal elections and seated defeated candidates who promised a more favorable response to royal policy than properly elected ones. The guilds also were unable to regulate themselves without royal mediation. Conflicts over jurisdiction arose between guilds practicing overlapping trades. Within guilds, masters of the trade often established discriminatory working conditions and pay for apprentices and journeymen, and created a closed hereditary succession to master status. The king was called upon as arbiter of disputes, both within the guilds and in their relations with other guilds.

Yet the continuing power and potential for autonomy in Paris became apparent when the state weakened, as it did late in the sixteenth century after several generations of religious antagonism between French Catholics and Protestants. In 1588, elements of the urban merchant notables led a successful rebellion against the weakened royal authority of Henry III (Valois), who was forced to flee the city. The king's power in the countryside was compromised by nobles grown powerful and independent due to royal favor, and a period of near anarchy ensued during which royal authority over Paris was not immediately reinstated. Instead a fully independent municipal government was established and remained in power until 1594, when Henry IV (Bourbon) entered the city. His reign was the first step in the rise of an autocratic dynasty that eventually achieved complete control of the city.

The subsequent process of decay in urban autonomy and the growth of royal administration in city affairs proceeded on two fronts. Henry IV and subsequent Bourbon kings stripped away the authority of the municipal government. The French king began to control the police, the criminal courts, the press, and the sermons in the city. Royal power extended to control over begging and prostitution as well as aid to the sick, the poor, and the victims of calamity. The urban government lost its authority to guard the city walls, to fix fountains and repair streets, and to supervise urban construction. Royal officials ordered streets cut through Paris for facilitating the passage of carriages. They tore down sheds and shops encroaching on the public way. Book censorship and the issuance of municipal bonds also passed into royal hands. Even election to the bureau de ville became an aspect of royal power, for the king refused to administer the oath of office to anyone whom he did not trust to follow royal dictates. So much a relic had Parisian civic institutions become that Louis XIV redrew the ward boundaries in order to sit new people in the municipal bureau.

The demise of Parisian autonomy was also accomplished by absorption of the merchant notables into the state bureaucratic system. The concept evolved that the highest ranks of Parisian merchants could be ennobled by their occupation of royal offices. This "nobility of the gown" (*noblesse de la robe*, as distinct from the hereditary nobility) achieved such offices by purchase from the king. Urban commercial wealth was thus harnessed to royal power; and merchant notables, who might have formed a subsidiary power group within Paris, were transformed into relatively innocuous state bureaucrats competing with the hereditary nobility instead of resisting the king. Among these newly ennobled urban merchants, a national identity and loyalty to the royal power replaced identification with Paris. Increasingly, they differentiated themselves from the trade and artisan guild associations of the city by careful marriage alliances, by purchase of country estates as charters for their new nobility, and by assumption of the life-style and ideology of the nobility.

As the city became less and less autonomous, as it grew to be administered by the king, its position increased as a center of sophistication, and state power and ceremony. New ideologies and religious associations formed in Paris and increasingly differentiated the urban style of life from the life-style of its rural environs. As a result of the Counter-Reformation, new monastic orders were subsidized, and a more pious Catholicism was adopted by the urban elite. A heroic image of the nobility emerged, one that accentuated an artistic and courtly life-style rather than the former virtues of the militant and often violent knight. The urbane image of the noble gentlemen superseded the rustic definition of life-styles—another point of separation between rural ways and the urban realm. A new architectural image of the city replaced the helter-skelter urban pattern inherited from the Middle Ages. French kings subsidized or promoted construction of squares in the city and planned to change the image of the city by opening it architecturally. The Place Royale and the Place Dauphine introduced the concept of vistas and the Baroque "cult of the street."[14] Majesty and grandeur became appurtenances of the city, and a few model projects conveyed an elite and idealized version of a splendid city amidst Paris's actual squalor, overcrowding, and poverty.

Tokugawa Castle Towns

Castle towns in Tokugawa Japan arose from the political centralization accomplished by the daimyos and shogun. Their construction, size, and prosperity heavily depended on the power and prestige of the particular lord who underwrote their existence. These cities served as the administrative centers and "integrative mechanism" for the new political order that emerged in the seventeenth century. Early castle towns appeared on hilltops that provided good defensive locations. Later with increasing pacification, they were constructed in open plains

---

[14]E.A. Gutkind, *International History of City Development*, Volume V: *Urban Development in Western Europe: France and Belgium* (New York: The Free Press of Glencoe, 1970), p. 78.

that possessed strategic military location, good communication facilities, and commercial possibilities. In these nascent cities, daimyos concentrated all the elements of control they possessed over society, wealth, and ritual. Just as daimyos were obliged to reside in the shogun's capital, so the daimyos' "feudal" subordinates, their samurai, were obligated to settle in the castle towns. The removal of the warriors from the countryside to the city neutralized a potential threat to the daimyos and further centralized the political system. Another consequence was to enrich the castle town by forcing the warriors to expend their grain allotments from the rural peasantry in the urban locale.

Merchants also settled in the new castle towns. Sometimes they came voluntarily, attracted by the economic opportunities arising from the daimyo's court and the offer of tax inducements and protection. At other times, merchants were forcefully resettled in castle towns by daimyos who wished to keep commercial wealth under scrutiny. Like the concentration of warriors in the city, merchant settlement increased the castle town's commercial prosperity as it impoverished the rural areas.

Temples and shrines were also relocated in the castle towns, often as a result of the daimyo's decree. Because these religious institutions were strongly built, daimyos located them at the city's periphery, where they formed an initial defense line for the urban area.

Centralization of political power, military forces, commerce, and religious institutions sharply demarcated the urban sphere from surrounding rural areas and promoted an urban life-style greatly removed from the world of the peasant cultivator. The shogun and daimyos accentuated the impoverishment of the rural countryside through legislation that restricted the peasant's freedom of action at the same time that it promoted the castle town's prosperity. Roads were constructed that made the various castle towns the centers of communication and transportation for their regions. The peasant could not barter his staple crops for craft goods, nor could he leave the rural area without a passport from the local ruler. Trade was allowed only to serve the castle town's prosperity, and merchants were forbidden to live in the rural areas or transact business except in the daimyo's city. Peasants were enjoined to live sober and pecunious lives, perhaps the only kind possible when the daimyo extracted forty to fifty percent of rural productivity in taxes.

Tokugawa rulers and their political dependents applied the same rigid social proscriptions to the populations of the castle towns. Sumptuary regulations and urban spatial organization reflected the major social distinctions between samurai military elite and the remaining urban dwellers, or townsmen (*chonin*). The samurai represented a majority of the urban population (generally ranging from fifty to eighty percent, but sometimes considerably less in commercial cities such as Osaka) and was its most prestigious component. The highest ranking warriors lived in a segregated quarter of the city with the castle fortifications and the shogun's or daimyo's palace at its center. Proximity to the castle indicated a warrior's relative status. Cooks, pages, and other service personnel of the warriors also resided in this quarter. This area formed the nucleus of the castle town and was usually protected by a wall or other defensive fortifications. Lower ranking warriors lived in a compact settlement at the very periphery of the castle town, a location that made them the first line of urban defenses.

Artisans, merchants, and the mass of the urban poor lived in the remainder of the city. The largest merchants—wholesalers and warehousemen—rivalled the warriors in splendor and luxury; but the majority of townsmen were traders, craftsmen, and newly urbanized peasants serving as apprentices or employees in shops. The urban lower class was continually replenished by an influx of peasants from the rural areas. These peasants were driven to the city by the lack of economic opportunities in the countryside. A hereditary class of outcasts, the *eta*, lived on the outskirts of the castle town and engaged in degrading occupations such as leatherwork. The eta also served as executioners and a state-controlled paramilitary force, reminiscent of the young men's gangs in Mamluk cities. A criminal class of thieves, sexual deviants, and the mentally deranged also resided on the urban fringe. The residential areas of townsmen were separated by numerous gates (107 in Hiroshima), which when closed at night restricted access to the various urban quarters or streets. They symbolized the sharp divisions in wealth and status within the urban area. Although the city as a social institution was sharply demarcated from the rural countryside, its internal cohesion rested almost entirely on the power and administration of its resident warrior elite.

Urban dependency on the warrior class is most evident in the form of municipal government. City administration rested with a town governor, drawn from the warrior class and appointed by the daimyo or shogun. Although councils of leading urban merchants existed, the town governor had final control over all administrative, police, and judicial functions in the city. The merchant councils and below them the numerous headmen drawn from the city's quarters acted mainly as passive transmitters of the elite's decrees and as collectors of data on the urban population required by the ruling power. Townsmen serving in city government were thus little more than state bureaucrats carrying out the daimyo's orders. Since property ownership was a qualification for positions on urban councils, the great mass of the city population was excluded from even this minimal involvement in civic affairs. City government in Tokugawa Japan therefore existed as a specialized administrative branch of the state for convenience in managing the large urban masses.

Only one segment of the urban population posed any threat to the dominance of the shogun or daimyo and the warrior class. Yet this population, the large-scale merchants, could not simply be eliminated by decree or force, because they provided important services for the warriors and the castle towns. From these two conflicting aspects of the commercial class arises the great ambivalence with which the Tokugawa regime treated the merchant community of the city. Legally and ideologically, merchants were relegated to the lowest status in society because they produced nothing and were merely commercial predators. Merchants had no political power, no rights as a class, and no legal protection for their property. When the Tokugawa regime judged such a course to be beneficial to national interests, it could invalidate coinage in common circulation and thus impoverish in one blow great numbers of merchants. Forced sales, unpaid loans, and confiscations were other practices by which the ruling elite continually proclaimed the merchant's political impotence and his dependence on state favor and protection.

In spite of these restrictive and oppressive conditions, merchants prospered throughout the Tokugawa regime at the expense of the warrior class. Their growing riches depended on the two indispensable functions they performed within the castle town: converting "tax rice" collected by the warriors from the peasants into money; and accumulating wealth through trade, which provided a necessary source of revenue for the shogun or daimyos. Tokugawa merchants, like their counterparts in Mamluk cities, controlled the distribution process and exchange system that permitted the warrior elite to gain money in exchange for their agricultural exactions from the peasantry. Merchants also offered warriors loans to offset the seasonality of their agriculturally-based incomes. Given the requirements of urban residence in capital and castle towns and the resulting status display and conspicuous consumption of the warriors, the merchants were an unavoidable although generally despised segment of the urban population.

Merchants were also indispensable to the Tokugawa regime for the wealth they could generate from trade—wealth that the elite harnessed to the power of the state and the maintenance of their privileged positions in administrative castle towns. In the early period of Tokugawa rule, restrictions on regional and national commerce were removed. A free policy of trade was instituted to draw merchants into the castle towns and to promote a commercial prosperity that could be taxed by the ruling elite. Cities such as Osaka developed whose primary urban function and predominant urban population were commercial. Yet the development of sources of wealth alternative to peasant agriculture posed great threats to the stability of the regime. Foreign influences (mainly European) entering through the port cities were another threat. The affluence of the merchants became increasingly noxious, especially as the purchasing power of the warriors' stipends decreased and the warrior class became more and more indebted to the large urban merchants. Although the weight of power always lay with the daimyo and shogun, merchants in peak periods of prosperity threatened to upset the status system and, through bribes and loans, to garner some degree of political autonomy. The ruling elite reacted by allowing trade to be monopolized, by confiscating merchant fortunes, by prohibiting suits for loan recovery, and by restricting foreign trade and regulating prices and commodity supply. Yet at the end of the Tokugawa period, merchants were still influential and wealthy, and the state administration was increasingly short of funds. Commercial enterprise became more and more individualistic, especially in provincial areas where the traditionalism and monopolism of the old merchant families were not so powerful and where the state elite was not so effective in its control of trade.

Parallel with the competition for prominence between warrior elite and urban merchant was the emergence of a new urban ideology that reflected the aspirations and attitudes of the commercial classes. Because of its primary commercial orientation, Osaka was the center of a developing humanism that emphasized the common man and his desires for advancement. Many schools were built to provide education demanded by the merchants, and literature and the arts also reflected new attitudes toward the status system of the country. The military elite strongly opposed this developing urban ideology as inimical to the traditional status system and as a threat to the priorities established by the regime. The struggle between the traditional status system and the new ideology of the townsmen continued throughout the later Tokugawa period with periodic successes for one or the other viewpoint. The final resolution came only after 1858, when Japan under a new regime was opened to foreign influences and embarked on a course of industrialization.

URBAN ORGANIZATION

The previous material indicates how the internal organization of administrative cities replicates the interaction of the ruling power with its peasant producers. Because the ruling elite reside in the city, the power they control and the wealth they consume become attributes of the administrative city. Religious institutions also adopt urban locations, either to enjoy the protection and subsidy of the elite (as in the Mamluk Near East), to gain access to the wealth of urban merchants (as in Paris), or to occupy the urban locations forced upon them (as in Tokugawa castle towns). Just as the state elite is sharply differentiated from rural cultivators in terms of status, wealth, and power, so too is the administrative city superior to its rural environs. The concentration of state political functions, elite expenditure, and ideological institutions in the city separate it from the peasant countryside.

State power and urban settlement form a single, supportive institutional pattern in the societies under discussion. Very often in dealing with peasant communities in such societies, anthropologists have described the political process with which the peasant must cope as being based on domination from the city. Such descriptions create the misleading impression that urban settlements inherently oppress their surrounding countryside and that superordination-subordination relations are necessary qualities of cities. To take this position is to confuse the power of the state with the nature of the urban locale. In bureaucratic state societies and their administrative cities, state power and urban settlement are indeed coterminous—but in other forms of states and other types of cities this equation would not hold true.[15]

Unlike regal-ritual cities, administrative cities are sharply distinguished in urban organization from the countryside by possession of a stable, occupationally specialized, and often very large population. This nonagricultural demographic base that separates city from peasantry is in large measure a by-product of the state ruling power. Major components of the urban populace are military cadres and bureaucratic functionaries who protect and administer the state, and merchants and artisans who provide the luxury goods and services required by the elite. A lower class of menials and day laborers and an outcast group of thieves, prostitutes, and other "undesirables" also constitute elements of the urbal population. Although they may not be the direct servitors of the ruling elite, the lower class also owes its urban location to the state. The constant influx to the city of impoverished peasants who supply cheap labor is the urban equivalent of the rural peasant whose agriculture is heavily taxed by state authorities.

Because their populations are large and heterogeneous in occupation, behavior and wealth, and because these populations are important sources of protection, labor, and wealth for the state, administrative cities must be managed. Two levels of social control and internal cohe-

[15]Cf. Eric Wolf's comments on this point in *Peasants* (Englewood Cliffs, New Jersey: Prentice-Hall, Inc., 1966), pp. 10–12.

sion exist in such cities, one dependent on state supervision (often in the form of a municipal government), the other based on ethnic, familial, religious, and occupational associations, In neither case does the city develop as a unified community with a corporate legal existence apart from the state. Instead, administrative cities remain disparate collections of different and distinct populations. These populations coexist harmoniously to the extent that state power suppresses internal dissension arising from social heterogeneity and wealth differentials; and they owe allegiance at most to cohesive groups based on neighborhood, kinship, occupational brotherhood, or ethnicity.

The large and heterogeneous urban population (other than the state bureaucracy and the military), while necessary to the state's functions, nevertheless posed threats to the stability of the social order in several ways (discussed later). The municipal government that operated informally in Mamluk cities and formally in Tokugawa castle towns and seventeenth-century Paris existed almost entirely to facilitate state domination of its administrative urban centers. In this sense, administrative cities were also administered cities, in that their populations, like the rural peasants, were given little or no initiative or autonomy in urban affairs. Although municipalities were found in Tokugawa Japan and seventeenth-century Paris, and although they may have been staffed by townsmen who stood apart from the ruling elite, city officers were in actuality delegates of the state. Their official roles and authority emanated from the state rather than from the city as an autonomous political realm. The distinction between "citizens" and mere townsmen that existed in Paris and Japan only served to eliminate most of the (propertyless and lower class) urban population from participation in even these state-derived municipal governing bodies.

The basic organizing principle in regal-ritual cities and segmentary state societies was ascriptive or quasi-ascriptive connection—whether the kin connections of the Rajputs and the Swazi, the fealty of Charlemagne and his magnates, or the percolation of the divine throughout Southeast Asian society. The use of ascription as a binding force also appears in administrative cities but with a greatly restricted scope. The social hierarchy is too pronounced, the wealth and status inequalities too obvious for such devices to join the entire population into a cohesive unit. Instead, such cohesiveness is only found in the city's quarters, in its families or occupational associations, in its wards of thieves and outcasts, in its young men's gangs and localized religious institutions. Once outside these, the cohesion of the administrative urban place depends on how efficiently the state administers it and how well the ruling elite impress their authority in the interests of continued urban existence. That is why the religious notables in Mamluk cities welcomed whatever state power proved triumphant, and that is why the Parisians bowed before Henry IV after periods of open rebellion.

Yet the urban populace is not completely the tool of the state elite, nor is the administrative city solely a settlement for convenience in administering the peasant countryside. Administrative cities pose problems to state elites because they possess oppressed and potentially contentious lower class populations, and because they contain populations with sources of wealth independent of peasant agriculture and therefore somewhat removed from state control. Lower class discontent arising from high grain prices, excessive taxation, and other social maladies is an ever present factor in all the state societies discussed in this chapter. Such lower classes are characteristically recent migrants to the city and are only minimally integrated into the urban social pattern except as exploited labor.

To counteract the potential disruption threatened by lower class violence, the state creates buffers to cushion the antagonism directed at it. The religious notables and market inspectors in Mamluk cities, the municipal governments in sixteenth-century Paris and Tokugawa Japan, are the first to absorb the ire of the impoverished townsmen. They are also, however, the natural leaders of urban discontent. Administrative cities thus have informal or institutionalized social brokers who act as middlemen between the demands of the state and the (potentially hostile) reactions of the urban populace. Such middlemen, usually drawn from the wealthy urbanites, look upward to the state for reflected glory and delegated authority, but they also look downward to the popular support of their fellow townsmen. They must effect a continuous balance between the conflicting interests of the state and the urban populace in the absence of both real power and a city-wide community allegiance at their disposal. Should this balance be upset, these urban brokers are the first to be punished by the state or to be taken as victims by an urban mob.

The state also counteracts the potential violence of the lower classes by channeling their hostilities in suitable directions. The young men's associations of Mamluk cities and the outcasts of Tokugawa castle towns are integrated as paramilitary auxiliaries into state domination. Lower class antagonism and violent response to economic and political oppression are redirected into military service deemed safe and productive for society. This is a mechanism of social control that we can still witness today in the treatment of the ethnic poor in American industrial cities.

The lower class challenge to state power is usually fitful, ill-organized, and possessed of limited goals. Its greatest chances for success come in periods when the state power is already weakened through loss of control over the peasant countryside or when the state stands threatened by other polities bent on conquest. However, a different kind of threat to the bureaucratic state is merchant wealth. This threat is constant and often highly organized. Merchant wealth undermines the basic social pattern of bureaucratic state society because it introduces economic autonomy into the urban area. Although merchants and commercial wealth are important adjuncts of the state, they are also potential threats, for their affluence and influence stem from sources outside peasant agriculture and therefore peripheral to direct state control.

An ongoing dialogue exists in the bureaucratic state and administrative city between state power and merchant wealth as they affect the internal organization of the urban sphere. The merchant needs the state as consumer of his services and supplier of basic agricultural commodities, as protector of trade routes, and as guarantor of internal urban and external peasant political stability to make trade possible on a large scale. The state needs the merchant for access to necessary funds, for luxury goods, and for the conversion of peasant grain into money. At times, the state suppresses and oppresses the merchant class and subjects trade to political requirements. In Japan, merchants were accorded the lowest social status, in direct contrast to the power their wealth provided them. In Mamluk cities, merchants continually were faced with forced purchases, oppressive taxation, and state confiscation. In other situations, the merchant has more autonomy and commercial license, and the state merely absorbs trading wealth and personnel into its political organization. The French state accomplished this through sale of royal offices to merchants (a kind of confiscation of merchant wealth to which the merchants willingly acquiesced), through replacement of their Parisian loyalties with national ones, and through the transformation of their bourgeois identification to noble status.

Even though commerce and the merchant are always the handmaidens of the state (although to a less thorough degree than is the peasant), variation in state-merchant relations determines the range of secondary urban variability found within the primary type of administrative city. The case material compares and contrasts several arrangements along this axis of merchant wealth and state authority, ranging from the almost complete suppression of the merchant in Mamluk cities, through the shifting imbalance in Tokugawa castle towns, and finally into the Parisian urban situation, where the merchant becomes a valuable agent in the growing centralization and wealth of the state.

Yet at no point does merchant wealth and concomitant urban economic autonomy exist outside the political context and without the franchise of the ruling power. Wealth alone brings the merchant nothing more than fears of confiscation, unpaid loans, and forced purchases. Only when the state decides to absorb new populations into the nascent

bureaucracy as in economic and political strategy does wealth lead to
status advancement in the social hierarchy. This conflict between the
ruling elite and merchant elements also gains expression in the internal
ideology of administrative cities.

URBAN IDEOLOGY

As the bureaucratic state strips the peasant of produce, so the
administrative city denudes the countryside culturally and ideologically.
The urban sphere increasingly forms a realm of cultural expression and
life-style separated from and superior to the peasant countryside. The
grandeur of monumental state architecture, the splendor of the arts, the
sophistication of religion in the city, form what Redfield called a "Great
Tradition" sharply removed from the folk or little traditions of the rural
peasantry. This urban-rural differentiation, however, does not signify a
complete cultural divide in ideology and life-style. It is a matter of
separation, not the result of one set of values antagonistic to another (as
will characterize urban-rural relations in the following chapter). Starting
from the same basic cultural premises, city and village develop value
orientations and life-ways that differ greatly in elaboration and sophistication and that maintain their separation even when they pass from
one sphere to the other. The religion of Paris is a more rarefied and
ascetic version of village Catholicism. Islam gains its full expression in
the urban context of the Near East. Motifs from the sophisticated city
filter into the countryside, but their form is greatly simplified in the
adjustment to the rural life-way. New beliefs may also arise in the rural
peasant world and be adopted in the city, but only after they have been
purified of many folk elements and elaborated to fit the sophistication of
the urban zone.[16]

In industrial state societies, rural-urban differences also obtain, and
popular stereotypes contrast city slicker and rural innocent or urban
greenhorn and rural handyman. Yet the separation in life-style and
belief pattern between urban and rural in industrial societies is not of the
same order as the separation in bureaucratic state societies. There the
city and peasant worlds are basically similar; they differ greatly in degree. In industrial state societies, a sophisticated communication and

---

[16]McKim Marriott has referred to these processes as "parochialization" and "univer-
salization" respectively. See "Little Communities in an Indigenous Civilization" in *Village
India: Studies in the Little Community*, McKim Marriott, ed. (Chicago: University of Chicago
Press, 1955), pp. 197–201.

transportation system, an all-pervasive market economy, a national political structure, and national allegiance integrate rural farmer and urban worker into a common framework. This framework is economic, political, and in large measure ideological. By contrast, urban-rural distinctiveness in the societies represented in this chapter was of the nature of two distinct worlds—separate in space and in custom. Administrative cities and their rural countrysides were effectively linked mainly in an interactional sense by state exploitation of the peasantry. They were separated in ideological terms by the variation in life-style that this exploitation underwrote in the city.

In what way did this ideological separation, the discontinuity of urban from rural, condition the spatial plan of the administrative city? Outside of the more compacted housing conditions that result from the urban density of population, administrative cities differ from rural villages mainly as reflections of the state. Gates, walls, castles, moats, citadels, and other state edifices form the core of administrative cities and represent a realm of life different from the rural world as surely as sumptuous regalia, the ideology of elite status, and other trappings of rank mark the rulers from the peasants. In terms of spatial design, the city is as much a city, as much distinctive in "look" from rural environs, as the state elite wish. Lacking community spirit and internal sources of authority, administrative cities depend on state power to construct monumental buildings, repair city fortifications, maintain public works and roads, and endow religious and educational institutions. If the state is weak or improvident, if the local state representative is miserly or not public spirited, the city suffers. Then the urban area comes closer to being merely a more densely settled version of the countryside.

The ideology of administrative cities embodied in urban space thus basically reflects the prestige of the state ruling elite. But other ideologies exist in the administrative city that challenge the primacy of the elite view, even though they have little impact on urban spatial design. Merchants and their independent wealth make urban organization something more than the structure of the bureaucratic state. They also make urban space something more than a mere reflection of state prestige. Their town houses, markets and shops, and guild halls, to the extent that they symbolize a commercial orientation rather than act solely as functional tools of it, reflect a different ideology—one intrinsic to the city and derived entirely from the urban experience. The merchant's view represents a less ascriptive and more pragmatic approach to the world. The Tokugawa merchant's humanism and pursuit of Western science, the Mamluk trader's defense of the rule of law and agitation against unjust state demands, the Parisian guildsman's pursuit of occupational autonomy, all testify to ideological currents separate from elite norms. Their presence in administrative cities establishes another model of urban life, one that has little expression in monumental state buildings or urban religious edifices. This is so because merchants have little power to impress their ideology in the spatial organization of the city (just as their power to transform urban organization is greatly restricted by the state). However, such a development does occur in the mercantile cities discussed in the following chapter.

The agency and ideology of the bureaucratic state in urban spatial design are most apparent in the urban planning that emerges (to varying degrees) as typical of administrative cities. A great range exists in the extent and effectiveness of urban planning in the societies under discussion, a variation that reflects both state power and specific cultural values. In general, however, whatever planning does occur comes as a result of state involvement in the urban sphere. Thus the Tokugawa daimyo arranged his castle, temples, and population to afford maximum protection in his town; the Mamluk emir subsidized public works and oversaw street clearance to maintain his status position. Seventeenth-century Paris affords the best example of urban planning. Although the Parisian royal plazas were undertaken on a grander scale than state planning in Mamluk cities or Tokugawa towns, royal images of Paris reflected the same social order as planning in other places. These royal plazas represent small particles of an elite urban space. They were constructed at state direction within the great mass of the foul, uncared-for, disease-producing, crowded streets of administrative cities and in the midst of the markets and houses of a suppressed merchant form.

The communication functions, demography, class structure, commercial activity, municipal government, and urban architecture of administrative cities depend on the power of the state and its urban allocation of wealth gained from a subservient peasantry. The city exists in adaptation to a highly centralized state regime administered by an elite on the one hand, and to a culturally and economically denuded peasant countryside on the other. Interactional links between city and rural environs rest on this unequal and oppressive political relationship; ideological links are discontinuous and create relatively discrete urban and rural worlds with little understanding and often less sympathy for each other. The adaptation of the administrative city to the wider society makes the city an integrative center for state power over the countryside. This function makes the city a locale for state administration, a market for luxury goods, a destination for impoverished ruralites, and a heterogeneous, dense settlement of population. These city populations cohere around state authority on the one hand and ethnic, familial, and religious associations on the other. The only effective and constant source of power outside the state elite is wielded by wholesalers, long distance merchants, grain dealers, and money changers. They tap or manipulate sources of wealth other than peasant agriculture, but their mercantile activities are always subject to state intervention and definition—and therefore do not lead to urban economic autonomy. Otherwise, in internal governance, demographic pattern, ideology, and form, the administrative city is mainly an extension of the bureaucratic state. It has little urban integrity, legal identity, and military protection, and few economic resources save those delegated by state power.

The portrait of administrative cities could be greatly expanded by inclusion of Imperial China, Mughal India, and many other "traditional" societies in which such cities obtained.[17] Yet even the limited material on Mamluk, Bourbon, and Tokugawa urbanism presented in this chapter indicates that the city type associated with strong state power and external economic dependency performs primarily administrative functions within the larger society. The internal organization and ideology of these urban places are equally reflective of the bureaucratic states in which they are set. The following chapter discusses a very different type of preindustrial urbanism—one in which adaptive conditions favor the primacy of merchant wealth, civic autonomy, and achieved social mobility over external domination of the city by the state.

[17]Cf. Rhoads Murphey, "The City as the Center of Change: Western Europe and China" in *Readings in Cultural Geography*, Philip L. Wagner and Marvin W. Mikesell, eds. (Chicago: University of Chicago Press, 1962).

5

Mercantile Cities
and City-States

A spirit of independence and autonomy, a desire for innovation, a predilection for social status based on achievement rather than birth, and a sense of community beyond the family or kin group are characteristics often associated with the city. In this view, urban places become centers of social change, economic development, and personal freedom in contrast to conservative, ascriptive, and traditional rural settlements. Cities are thus perceived as sources of novel economic and productive arrangements and new political orders that challenge the fabric of society. Regal-ritual cities and administrative cities clearly do not conform to this vision of the urban experience. Therefore, the city whose "air makes man free" and whose constitution makes them (somewhat) equal is only one type of urban locale among many. The objective of this chapter is to elucidate the type of preindustrial city whose system of social stratification, pattern of social mobility, and relative autonomy from the rest of society put it at sharp remove from the types of preindustrial urbanism previously discussed. By specifying under what conditions and in what sort of state society such "mercantile cities" (as we will term them) occur, this chapter attempts an exposition and explanation of the city as center of change and sphere of enlightenment.

Perhaps because of their importance in the development of the Western tradition, perhaps because of the relatively copious amounts of data available on them, the cities of the European Middle Ages and those of the ancient classical world—exemplars of the mercantile urban type— have been given special weight in the development of ideas about the nature of urbanism. Only the cities of the industrial world have gained more attention and attracted more scholarly research. As a result, characteristics or qualities associated with medieval European cities and ancient Greece and Rome are often given a prominence and a universality that detract from a balanced judgment of their relevance for the development of cities in human society.

The opposite reaction—dismissal of the urbanism exemplified by medieval Europe and Antiquity—is equally dangerous. Sjoberg, for example, treats medieval European urban patterns as temporary and unusual variants of his "preindustrial city" model, a position for which he has been soundly criticized.[1] Indeed, the cities discussed in this chapter do not fit neatly into the Sjoberg thesis. But rather than dismissal as unique and shortlived deviations, such cities warrant treatment as important variants of urbanism—variants that develop, endure, and disappear under economic and political conditions that need to be specified. Several influential urban theorists, among them the economic historian Henri Pirenne and the sociologist Max Weber, have adopted just this goal. Although we may reject their ethnocentric notions that the city represented by Antiquity or medieval Europe is the only or most significant urban type (as we did in Chapter Four with Sjoberg's universal application of his "preindustrial" model), nevertheless their analyses will help illuminate another primary type of urbanism.

One of the best known and most influential theories about cities and their origins suffers from this undue emphasis on the characteristics of what is in fact only a single urban type. Henri Pirenne investigated the re-emergence of cities in Europe after the Dark Ages, which followed the fall of the Roman Empire. In pursuit of this goal, Pirenne naturally developed a definition of the city—one that has continued to influence judgments up to the present day about what is and what is not truly urban. The city in the European Middle Ages arises, according to Pirenne, because it is a waystation for international trade and traders. Commercial activities, purchase, and sale bring men together in newly formed urban environments that coalesce around the protected residence of a bishop or around the fortified castle of a feudal lord. These latter settlements (which constitute regal-ritual cities as described in Chapter Two) do not constitute cities in Pirenne's view. They lack the two characteristics that Pirenne sees as fundamental qualities arising in

---

[1]Gideon Sjoberg, *The Preindustrial City, Past and Present* (New York: The Free Press, 1960), p. 69. For criticism, see Sylvia Thrupp, "The Creativity of Cities: A Review Article," *Comparative Studies in Society and History,* IV, 1 (1961), pp. 60–63.

his commercial cities: an urban bourgeoisie, or middle class, that depends on trade for its wealth and political autonomy from feudal power-holders; and a communal organization of the urban citizenry that creates a municipal integrity in order to free the city from control by local feudal lords or religious authorities.[2]

The presentation in this chapter of the mercantile city type will at many points concur with Pirenne's analysis of European medieval cities (even though we obviously do not accept the mercantile city as the only form of the city). Unlike Pirenne's thesis, however, this presentation does not view international trade as the sole formative factor in mercantile cities (local trade and money-lending were also important), nor does it conceive such cities as completely detached from the power structure of the surrounding state society. Our presentation will attempt to analyze more adequately the importance of trade in such cities and their relations with the states in which they are set.

Another theory of great consequence in urban scholarship has been Max Weber's contrast of "Oriental" with "Occidental" urbanism. Weber believed that only settlements that formed urban communities constituted true cities, a situation that obtained almost exclusively in the Occident and even there only for short periods in ancient and medieval times. Weber's analysis of the Occidental city parallels Pirenne's exposition of medieval European urbanism, although it does not rest solely on the causative agency of international trade. According to Weber, five attributes define the urban community: It must possess (1) a fortification, (2) a market, (3) a law code and court system of its own, (4) an association of the urban citizenry creating a unified urban populace and a sense of municipal integrity, and (5) at least partial political autonomy, so that those who govern the city are elected by the urban citizens.[3]

Oriental cities, Weber believed, rarely achieved these characteristics because they were more thoroughly supervised by state rulers, and because magical and religious barriers prevented the urban residents from forming an association of citizens with common interests and defenses against state control. Even in the Occident, true urban communities existed only for short periods of time, mainly in northern Europe. Weber, like Pirenne, thus sees the development of new social and economic classes and new urban political forms as characteristics of this historically and geographically limited city development. Many of the qualities Weber adduced for his Occidental city will also appear in our presentation of the mercantile urban type. However, we will attempt

[2]Henri Pirenne, *Medieval Cities: Their Origins and The Revival of Trade*, trans. by Frank D. Halsey (Princeton: Princeton University Press, 1925), p. 56.
[3]Max Weber, *The City*, trans. and ed. by Don Martindale and Gertrude Neuwirth (Glencoe, Illinois: The Free Press, 1958), pp. 54–55.

to show its existence for parts of the world other than the Occident, and thereby to specify the political and economic conditions under which it arose or might have arisen in any world region.

What then are the characteristics of the mercantile city pattern? This third type of preindustrial urbanism arises through a combination of political and economic factors in the larger society that concentrate wealth and power within the urban locale itself (see typology, pp. 33–36). Mercantile cities arise where political hegemony over a region is weak or absent, as during the periodic decay of bureaucratic states, or when only weakly centralized segmentary states obtain, *and* where a source of urban wealth and economic autonomy exists other than control over peasant subsistence agriculture. In some mercantile cities, wealth accrues to the urban population from long distance trade and money-lending. In others, riches arise through urban capital invested in rural land under share-cropping systems or from urban subsidy of exportable handicrafts such as pottery, metal, or woven cloth. Whatever the basis, the mercantile city is the primary source of wealth, accumulation of which is unhindered by the commercial restraints of a powerful state ruling elite. The city is a place for the production of riches, not just a consumption center where wealth squeezed from peasant labor is expended by state rulers, or where artisans congregate to supply the needs of resident state administrators. As mercantile cities become more economically autonomous or as the state society weakens further, urban locales increasingly imprint their own political and economic organization onto surrounding rural areas. This development, should it continue, eventually leads to a derivative urban type, the city-state, wherein the weakened state power is resurrected within the mercantile city.

COMMERCIAL AUTONOMY
AND MERCANTILE CITY

Mercantile cities develop within decentralized segmentary states, or during periods of dissolution within bureaucratic states, when no superior power can effectively control the military threat, political independence, and commercial growth of the nascent mercantile cities. This urban type may also arise when a weak ruler actually subsidizes autonomous urban growth as a potential source of revenue and followers against internal enemies. Some mercantile cities achieve only partial political autonomy from preexisting state rulers; some are completely absorbed by these rulers after a short period of autonomy; and only a few develop into full-fledged city-states. The greater the commercial enterprise controlled by the city and the less powerful preexisting state rulers are, the more the urban settlement can wrest autonomy from these state rulers. In such a situation the city can export its own political and economic organization into the countryside. The autonomy of mercantile cities is expressed by those qualities that Weber and Pirenne emphasized for medieval European cities: independent municipal government, urban fortifications and military forces with which to resist state rulers, and city law. Urban autonomy reaches its highest development when cities form self-contained legal associations whose economic privileges and monopolies are safeguarded by charters and legal covenants, and who are protected from state abuse. When completely outside the jurisdiction of state rulers, such urban places form "city-states." Such urban places act as nuclei of a new state order that originates within the city and its urban population and then engulfs surrounding rural areas.

Not all mercantile cities become city-states. Three situations may forbid such a development: (1) The forces of rural powerholders (for example, feudal nobility) may prove too strong; (2) an urban ruling elite may curtail civic government and co-opt commercial leaders (as happened in Paris under the Bourbon kings); and (3) the wealth of the city may be insufficient or too transitory to guarantee its resistance to external conquest. Thus, even when political and economic factors adventitiously combine to favor the mercantile city, their variable strength or weakness may imbalance the resulting pattern of urban adaptation.

Although weak, preexisting state power may not be so fragmented as to capitulate completely before the nascent mercantile center, under such conditions, mercantile cities can become at best legally autonomous corporations that play a more or less independent political role connected to the wax and wane of state power. A different imbalance may arise when the trade or investment of the mercantile city does not sufficiently guarantee its economic wealth independent of rural agriculture. In such circumstances, mercantile cities live under constant threat from rural powerholders or richer cities waiting to take advantage of their economic dependence.

In proper conjunction and balance, however, political instability in the state society and economic autonomy produce the quintessential mercantile urbanism, the city-state. Through its own economic resources and its own urban militia, the city comes to control an increasing rural territory along with the agricultural products and producers within it. The mercantile city expands to fill the political vacuum in the state society. In the process it is transformed into a city-state wherein urban laws, urban elites, and urban commerce provide the adjudication, the rulers, and the economics for all lands and people within its expanded boundaries.

The following material describes Toulouse, Padua, and Florence—medieval mercantile cities in the Southern Europe—and Japanese port cities and Javanese bazar towns. These cities represent the range possible in the autonomy achieved by mercantile cities: from absorption in a bureaucratic state order to independence as a city-state.

Medieval European States
and Mediterranean Cities

The dissolution of the Roman Empire, which led to a general political decentralization, also witnessed a severe recession in urban population and urban activities throughout Europe. The characteristic urban pattern of the ensuing Dark Ages rested primarily on the fortified regal-ritual centers of feudal magnates or ecclesiastic authorities. Beginning with the eleventh century, however, a regenerated or rejuvenated European urbanism developed with characteristics that set the urban centers at odds with feudal secular or religious powers. North of the Alps, the nascent urban settlements represented new urban developments that arose in response to the great commercial expansion and population growth of the late Middle Ages. In the Mediterranean region and especially Italy, Roman urban sites, atrophied in the Dark Ages and ruled as personal fiefs by secular or religious authorities, gained a new life as centers of trade or capitalist land ownership. No less than their northern counterparts, these renascent cities of the Mediterranean came to resist the suffocating powers of their feudal overlords. Such resistance in Italy and elsewhere led to the creation of city-states unlike anything found in northern Europe. [4]

The following case material begins with a capsule history of medieval Toulouse, a city in southern France that represents the evolution of

[4]For a general review of these developments, especially in northern Europe, see Fritz Rörig, *The Medieval Town* (Berkeley: University of California Press, 1967); E.A. Gutkind, *International History of City Development*, Volume I: *Urban Development in Central Europe* (New York: The Free Press of Glencoe, 1964); Robert S. Lopez, "The Trade of Medieval Europe: The South," in *The Cambridge Economic History of Europe*, Volume II: *Trade and Industry in the Middle Ages*, M.M. Postan, E.E. Rich, and Edward Miller, eds. (Cambridge: The University Press, 1963), pp. 257–354; H. Van Werveke, "The Rise of the Towns," in *The Cambridge Economic History of Europe*, Volume III: *Economic Organization and Policies in the Middle Ages*, M.M. Postan, E.E. Rich, and Edward Miller, eds. (Cambridge: The University Press, 1963); and A.B. Hibbert, "The Origins of the Medieval Town Patriciate," *Past and Present*, III (1953).

mercantile urbanism within a changing external political order. At times strong, but mostly weak, divided, and embattled, the preexisting state society of the region consisted of the county of Toulouse and its hereditary count. The state society was involved with the city in a fluctuating contest for supremacy. For a short period, the city gained the upper hand, won political autonomy and economic freedom, and attempted (by military conquest and subjugation of the count's territories) to create a totally independent city-state. In the end, Toulouse's march was stopped and its autonomy and freedom were stripped away because of a political rearrangement of the larger society, a rearrangement that strengthened the local ruler at the urban area's expense. The history of Toulouse thus illustrates the dynamic of mercantile cities in their relation to the state society: the city's prominence, independence, and imperialist policy when the state is weak; its subordination and containment when external political power is strong.

Toulouse

The city of Toulouse existed long before the medieval period.[5] Its site had been inhabited by Celts and later, Romans, and afterward became the capital of a Visigothic state and then the capital of the Carolingian realm of Aquitaine. In the eleventh century, the town served as a capital for the rulers of this part of southern France, the counts of Toulouse. During this century the city of Toulouse experienced an urban renaissance based on increasing commercial wealth and an expanding urban population of merchants and craftsmen. This urban growth coincided with a period of feudal crisis and political upheaval in southern France. Invasion by outside state powers from the North and the resulting embattled condition of the Toulouse counts allowed various parts of their domain to secede. Such conditions permitted rural and urban aristocrats to assert their independence from their feudal superior. The city of Toulouse was a center of the dissolving political power of the counts even though no urban community yet existed at Toulouse. Instead, the urban settlement and its inhabitants were territorially divided into one section called "the City," under the authority of a secular feudal ruler in the person of a viscount, and another section, "the Burg," which was controlled by ecclesiatic authorities.

Both the hereditary viscontal family and the ecclesiastics of Tou-

---

[5]Material on Toulouse is from John Hine Mundy, *Liberty and Political Power in Toulouse, 1050–1230* (New York: Columbia University Press, 1954).

louse had grown more powerful and independent as the realm of the Toulouse counts weakened. During the eleventh century as the decentralization of the realm continued, even more localized and less powerful feudal elements began to challenge their political superiors. An association of the wealthy and elite urban residents in Toulouse arose to challenge the viscount and ecclesiastic authorities. This association of Good Men, as they were called, was composed both of hereditary aristocratic families who lived in the city and urban merchants or landowners who owed their prominence to recently acquired wealth. Whether resident in the City or the Burg, these urban notables, or patricians, came together to pursue common political goals. Their alliance formed an urban community out of the disparate residential and political segments of the urban settlement.

To maintain control of the state against both external invaders and the larger internal feudal dissidents grown disorderly, the count of Toulouse was forced to ally and thus to recognize the association of Good Men. In 1119 the political tides changed in favor of the state rulers, the counts of Toulouse were restored to power, the church in the city was removed from secular affairs, and the viscontal family lost control over the urban sphere. The count's resistance to external enemies and his control over his larger feudal subordinates was consolidated. By the same token, the elite urban residents gained a real community organization apart from intermediary ecclesiastic and secular feudal overlords.

Throughout the twelfth century, the recurrent weakness of the counts and the ever present attacks from the North allowed the city of Toulouse to determine in great measure its own destiny. The city had an independent source of wealth through trade and an autonomous military force that was based on an urban militia drawn from the Good Men. This situation increasingly allowed it to impose its own political desires on the state power. The count of Toulouse gradually lost his control over urban taxation, his feudal requirements of military service, and his seignioral rights over trade. By 1175, twenty-four consuls drawn from the urban notables became the governing body of the now virtually autonomous city. At the end of the twelfth century, the count had lost all power to legislate for the city, although he could still reject the legislative acts of the consuls. The consuls, representing the urban notables, took over supervision of town property and roads, police duties, maintenance of fortifications, and even the purity of state mintage. Jurisdiction over murder cases, property destruction, sedition, and later personal injury and civil justice also passed from the count to the consuls.

The fortunes of the Toulouse count reached their nadir in 1189 when the city militia rose up and defeated him at a time when he was also heavily engaged in defending his patrimonial realm against northern French invaders. Important changes in the civic organization of the urban settlement ensued in the wake of this almost total success of the Toulouse notables against the count. Once the external enemy represented by the count was no longer a challenge to the city, internal political and economic factions—which had suspended their hostility before now—arose to threaten the unity of the urban community. By the end of the twelfth century, craft associations and trade fraternities of the less wealthy and less traditionally prominent families of Toulouse challenged the leadership and primacy of the original families of notables. This political dissent was not led by the city's poor, but rather by those relatively affluent citizens who were excluded from municipal government by the increasingly elitist and restrictive views of the original Good Men. Their existence and growing political demands indicated both the expanding population and the increasing commercial prosperity that Toulouse had experienced over the preceding century. The main demand of these newly affluent but not yet influential urbanites was a reform in city government.

Toulouse's twenty-four consuls were assisted in their civic deliberations by a common council, which by the end of the twelfth century had become a small, aristocratic body drawn from the same notable families as filled the consulships. In 1202, shortly after the ultimate exclusion of the count's power from the city, a popular party threw out this patrician civic government and instituted consular rule by newly wealthy and predominantly commercial interests. At roughly the same moment, the city of Toulouse set out on a military conquest of the surrounding countryside. The goal was to create urban dominion over a rural territory where feudal powerholders, trade restrictions, and all other impediments to the political and commercial preeminence of the city could be forcibly extricated. Thus, the now autonomous mercantile city, under the aggressive leadership of the popular movement, was attempting to become a city-state with a dependent territory of its own creation and conquest.

Invaders from northern France—in the Albigensian Crusade to root out heresy and usury in the South—conquered the city in 1216, reinstated the old notables (although with much reduced powers), and thus temporarily put an end to the city's military and political designs on the surrounding countryside. But the counts of Toulouse returned to battle the invaders, and in the ensuing period of political upheaval from 1218 to 1229, the city again won many concessions from its hereditary prince as the popular party once again determined its destinies. During this period the city stripped the hereditary count of his powers in return for its continued loyalty to him. This was done to such an extent that the count's campaign became merely a continuation of the city's previous expansionist policies.

The city's reinstated freedom was shortlived, however. After 1229, peace was made between the Toulouse count and the northern invaders. The reconstituted powers of the count and the hostile reaction of the region to the city's aggression immobilized the urban area. The old notable families, which in some cases had aligned with rural feudal magnates to thwart the city's expansion, returned to power, and a less revolutionary program was instituted. In 1249, the realm of Toulouse passed by hereditary succession to the brother of the French king. Freed from internal dissent and unthreatened by external enemies, the new count suppressed the liberties and autonomy of the city of Toulouse and curtailed its expansion. By 1271, when the Toulouse region was inherited by the king of France, the former autonomy of the city was already a relic. Its future history was to show the increasing royal supervision and penetration that we portrayed in the discussion of Paris in Chapter Four.

Many of the social arrangements, political developments, and civic dynamics briefly sketched for Toulouse also characterize northern Italian mercantile cities in the Middle Ages. In Italy, however, non-urban state authorities were even weaker and presented even less impediment to urban freedom and expansion. Italian cities, unlike Toulouse, became fully developed city-states—that is, the city achieved domination of its surrounding countryside. The following material on two Italian cities illustrates another variant of the relationship between mercantile city and state power. It also probes more deeply into the economic and political institutions that accompanied the city's rise to autonomy and statehood.

Padua

In 1320, the city of Padua contained at least thirty-five thousand people.[6] Urban wealth and population concentration depended neither on long-distance commerce nor on production of export commodities nor on international banking—activities that, as we will see, characterized the Florentine economy. Padua's existence was predicated on local money-lending and the interest (often declaimed as usurious) gained thereby. It also depended on the political subjugation and economic exploitation of the city's rural environs (*contado*) by landowners, land speculators, and rentiers resident in the urban settlement. Local trade

---

[6]The following materials are derived from J.K. Hyde, *Padua in the Age of Dante* (Manchester, England: Manchester University Press, 1966).

and distribution functions for the surrounding contado were also important additions to the city's wealth.

Padua's control over its contado was a vehicle for the extension of
urban money-lending and financial speculation into rural agriculture.
The city's contado began two miles from the center of the urban settlement and encompassed a territory whose boundaries roughly correspond to the modern Italian province of Padua. Most of the contado was
owned by city residents ranging from large hereditary magnates whose
rural properties had passed to them as feudal domains to newly prominent men whose purchase or lease of rural land grew out of profits
gained in local commerce or money-lending. Both these groups had
combined to form the Paduan commune and the patrician class, which
was the original mainstay of municipal government and urban political
autonomy. They lived in the city as absentee owners and rentiers from
the profits of their rural enterprise—an example of the manner in which
mercantile cities transformed the countryside to fit urban economic
dictates and organization.

Padua's political domination and economic reorganization of the
contado also determined the allocation of rural products, again to further urban consumption and affluence. The city commune restricted the
movement of all goods, from precious metals to dung, unless a tax was
paid to the municipality. The urban area performed distribution and
exchange functions for the entire region, and until the fourteenth
century Padua exported food products to the rest of Italy.

Because social mobility through wealth was possible, families rose
and fell, and therefore power and social status in Padua were ever-
changing. In the early period, leadership and eminence in the city went
to those men who possessed rural property and rural castles with which
they reinforced their dominance in the city. Such men formed the class
of urban notables (patriciate) and were considered noble or near-noble
in popular estimation. Throughout the twelfth and thirteenth centuries,
these original patrician families with an illustrious feudal past—that is,
the lesser feudal nobility that had originally wrested Padua from its
ecclesiastic overlords—were penetrated by urban money-lenders, land
speculators, and others whose wealth was of recent acquisition. After the
twelfth century, political influence became increasingly an urban phenomenon. It was lodged with various craft associations or guilds and the
lesser city tradesmen who had been excluded from city government
under patrician dominance. Beginning as a private association (like the
commune) of guilds to protect their commercial interests in an expanding urban economy, the *popolo* or popular movement in Padua soon
became an effective voice in civic government. The popolo partially
replaced and restricted the old patrician dominance. Its political goals

were to remove the entrenched patrician families from power and to make city government favor its commercial and more purely urban interests. Factionalism and violent quarrels within the old patriciate aided the popular cause. However, the rural power bases and fortified castles of the urban patriciate formed a continuing threat to the rule of the popolo in the city. Some notable families were so influential and their rural power so great a threat to the urban community that they were legally debarred from any role in civic government.

Yet the expanding population and commerce of the city, the volatile economic cycles that led some families to affluence and others to bankruptcy, and the overriding importance of wealth rather than hereditary status for social prominence meant that the distinction between patricians and popolo was not rigid. Many notable families had lost their wealth, and their reduced economic condition gave them little weight in urban affairs. Many other families were upwardly mobile and entered occupations, such as the law, or achieved social statuses, such as knighthood, that moved them into notable ranks. Even the lesser guildsmen might have their sons trained as notaries or scribes to facilitate their social advancement. As a man prospered, he or his children advanced socially. Commercial or craft wealth thus became joined to the achievement of a higher commoner or even patrician status in an evolving system of social stratification. This system permitted social recognition and political power to those who were successful.

The public arena in which this social advancement was expressed was municipal politics. Although the egalitarian ideal of modern industrial democracies was absent in Padua and other Italian city-states, civic government was nevertheless more open and popularly-based, and more responsive to purely urban needs, than that found in the administrative cities of bureaucratic states. Padua, like other northern Italian cities, underwent an evolution in civic government. This evolution saw the city electorate increasingly expanded and the civic government made increasingly responsible to the wishes of the less affluent. The original urban administration consisted of several consuls, or executive officers, drawn from a larger legislative council that contained the patricians of the city. Later, factional disputes between these notables led to the replacement of the consuls by a single *podesta,* who represented a foreign (non-Paduan) and supposedly apolitical administrative specialist. Early in the thirteenth century, the exclusiveness of the municipal government was sundered by the intervention of the popular movement. Rather than replacing the podesta and patrician council, the popolo augmented them with a new twelve-member council that became the seat of real power in the city. This council was selected every two months by elections in which all members of the popolo voted. Eight of its members were drawn from various urban guilds, and four came from each of the city's four wards. Although ostensibly representing the lower urban strata, government by the popolo was not fully democratic. It became a privileged association of the smaller traders and leading guildsmen among the urban populace. Excluded from membership in the popolo were those Paduans who were not members of any craft association or whose tax assessment was too low to qualify them for popolo membership. In all, ninety percent of the urban population had no direct voice in civic affairs. Further, the highest offices of the popolo were always reserved for the wealthiest and most prominent members. At most, the humbler folk of the city could hope to join some notable's faction and thus indirectly influence public policy. Patron-client relationships linking a wealthy political leader and lower status followers within the city organized (for the notable's purposes) the otherwise politically inchoate urban and contado poor.

Because Padua was not a great trade emporium or handicraft manufacturing center, the city heavily depended on the reorganization of rural agriculture by urban capital and urban investors. So too, the politics of the surrounding region greatly influenced city government and urban organization. The city was incessantly caught up in an overarching series of factional struggles among rural aristocrats, who tried to win Padua to their side and who attempted (often successfully) to dominate the city and enlist its resources in their quest for power and territorial dominion. Such a faction coalesced around a high-ranking rural aristocratic family that was attempting to impress its rule over an entire region and that was opposed by another similarly-constituted aristocratic faction. Below the premier family of a faction came several less influential notable families whose sphere was still wider than a single city. Still lower came lesser notable and wealthy families within a single city. Thus in Padua in any period, some patrician families followed and others opposed the aristocratic factions that were constituted on a regional level. The city was intimately bound to political conflict in the larger society, but at the same time it was an independent unit whose allegiance was valuable and sought after. Two extremes might result from the involvement of the urban center in regional political factions. The urban patrician faction that opposed the regional aristocratic faction might prevail, and the city's militias would be sent out to devastate (if possible) the rural aristocrat's castles and following—and thus remove his intrusion in urban affairs. His followers in the city usually met violent ends. The other alternative was for the city to be won over to the rural aristocrat's cause. In this case, the city indicated its inability to maintain its own freedom and it soon passed under the *signoria*, or despotic rule, of the aristocratic family.

In the heyday of the Italian mercantile cities, especially in powerful ones such as Florence, the former alternative was most common. Eventually, however, the signoria came to characterize the Italian urban pattern. Because of its limited commercial resources and its heavy dependence on rural powerholders, Padua very early succumbed to despotic rule. From 1237 to 1256, the city was ruled by the signoria, although urban liberties were restored when the city was retaken by exiled Paduan citizens. In 1318, after a disastrous war with the neighboring city of Verona, the city again passed under despotic rule, which continued until 1405. In that year, the city was absorbed into the growing city-state of Venice, and its loss of urban autonomy was complete.

Florence

Unlike Padua, the city of Florence was a center of long-distance trade, international banking, and manufactured cloth throughout the later Middle Ages and early Renaissance.[7] The city was a major emporium in the general wave of commerce that took Italian merchants throughout the Mediterranean, the Levant, the Black Sea region, and the North African coast. Florentine political autonomy and commercial freedom from feudal superiors had been gained by a coalition of lesser feudal aristocrats who owned estates in the city's contado and the descendants of rural traders who migrated to the city and invested in commerce and manufacture while still retaining land in the rural area. These two classes came together in Florence to form the patrician ruling group, which whether originally aristocrat or trader, became homogeneously (in comparison to Padua) involved in money-lending and banking, in subsidy of trade and manufactures, and in rural land investment and share-cropping. Eventually, this more thorough-going commercial ideology and greater focus on commercial activities within the city made Florence much more politically independent of (and often in control over) rural aristocratic factions than was Padua. The countryside existed as an extension of Florentine capitalist investment into agriculture rather than as a potential source of political power that might threaten to engulf the city. International banking and trade in Florence depended on a favorable political and economic relationship with the papacy and the kingdom of Naples, a relationship that was determined by the city rather than imposed by outside powers. Florentines monopolized papal bank-

---

[7]This description of Florence is based on Gene A. Brucker, *Renaissance Florence* (New York: John Wiley & Sons, Inc., 1969).

ing and tax collection and controlled the grain trade of the Neapolitan state. They also enjoyed trade outlets throughout northern Europe, the Mediterranean, and the Near East. Their functions as bankers and commodity dealers in foreign lands meant that Florentines often performed functions similar to those of merchants in administrative cities. However, Florentines avoided the restraints placed on traders in administrative cities because their political allegiance and commercial profits were taken up by their home city.

Another factor in Florentine prosperity—one that more clearly and completely gave it an urban pattern different from Padua's—was the woolen cloth industry. Raw wool from England and France was imported into Florence and there woven into cloth, which found a ready international market. Urban occupational structure, city population, and wealth were greatly dependent on this industry. Affluent and prestigious city dwellers, usually belonging to the class of notables, capitalized the weaving process, which depended on specialized artisan labor organized around a putting-out system. Spinners, weavers, fullers, dyers, and shearers each processed the wool in turn at home or in their own shops; managers and brokers represented the interests of the capitalists and oversaw the efficient coordination of all these disparate processes.

The general Florentine urban economy depended heavily on the cloth business, much as the automobile complex in the United States has engendered hosts of subsidiary services and occupations. Iron-mongers supplied tools for cloth workers; soapmakers were necessary to the woolwashers; dyemakers provided colorants; and craftsmen constructed looms, combs, spinning wheels, and other implements. This proliferation of artisans and cloth workers—an ill-paid and low ranked but numerically significant part of the Florentine population—was beholden to the urban notables who subsidized the industry.

The economic life of the city—trade, banking and manufacture—was reflected in the urban social hierarchy. Lawyers, international traders, and bankers enjoyed the highest status and greatest affluence. They composed the seven major guilds that were represented in the original patrician government of the city. Below them came fourteen lower guilds of artisans and shopkeepers who only gained access to civic offices after 1343. Much of the urban population—cloth workers, peddlers, laborers, servants, and beggars—were not organized in any association and had no voice in civic affairs.

Patrician landowners and rural aristocrats originally held political power in the city in its early days of independence from feudal overlords. Throughout the twelfth and thirteenth centuries, patrician ranks and civic government were broadened to include many newly wealthy urbanites; successful artisans, new merchants and manufacturers, and immigrants from the contado entered the ruling elite. The social mobility that existed in Padua also obtained in Florence—perhaps on a larger scale because of the greater weight given to international trade, banking, and manufacture in the Florentine economy. After 1343, a guild government like the popolo in Padua was instituted in Florence. The fourteen lesser guilds gained access to municipal affairs, although many other guilds were excluded and the large part of the laboring population that belonged to no guild was also unrepresented. Even earlier, the powerful aristocratic families with great rural properties and power bases had been denied political office in the city. Florence much more effectively than Padua negated the impact of rural powerholders on urban government. It instituted a wider franchise in the city among the purely commercial and artisan population.

With its great concentration of wealth and power, the city launched wars against neighboring cities such as Pisa, Fiesole, and Siena, which it eventually absorbed. The greatest threats to Florentine stability came from within the city rather than from the larger society. Factionalism within the patrician leadership was an unending source of discontent, political upheaval, personal vendettas, and secret maneuvering. The city was also continuously threatened by urban citizens who had been exiled when their political faction had lost power or when city leaders feared them as organizers of lower class discontent. Rusticated to the countryside or other cities, yet forever regarding Florence as their true home, such men could only dream of fomenting internal dissent or of leading a successful invasion of exiles with which to enter again their treasured city.

The ever-broadening political electorate in Florence saw a further (temporary) development in the devolution of power to the urban masses. This situation indicates how significantly Florence departed from more patrician Padua. In 1378, a factional dispute that had been brewing for many years within patrician ranks broke violently into the open. A discontented patrician group joined with disgruntled managers and subcontractors in the weaving industry and with the exploited urban laborers. They caused a series of eruptions involving civic strife, property destruction, and revolutionary social upheaval called the Ciompi uprising that fundamentally threatened the Florentine social order. Such violent revolts by the disfranchised and underprivileged city population also occurred in other medieval cities with large labor forces. These uprisings had many qualities of a proletarian revolt even though they were led by alienated patricians and popolo. In the wake of the Ciompi uprising, a revolutionary urban government was instituted in Florence. It guaranteed a fixed number of political offices to merchants, artisans, and laborers. This innovative civic constitution lasted only until

1382, when it was repressed and then replaced by a conservative patrician government, which evolved in an increasingly oligarchic way throughout the course of its tenure from 1382 to 1434. After a brief resumption of popular government, Florence in 1469 passed under the signoria of the Medici family.

Toulouse, Padua, and Florence corroborate Weber's belief that "true" urban communities were primarily Occidental developments. Yet if political instability in state societies coupled with urban economic autonomy are the conditions that give rise to mercantile cities, examples of this urban type should have appeared in non-European societies whenever and wherever such conditions obtained. Unfortunately, data are very limited on such urban developments in the Orient, partially because of the limited historical knowledge available for many areas and partially because of the prevalence of bureaucratic state organization throughout the region. The following cases indicate that mercantile cities outside the Occident did periodically arise under political and economic conditions similar to those in medieval Europe. In the societies discussed below, mercantile urbanism was shortlived and quickly subdued by the power of renascent bureaucratic states (although the longevity of European city-states should not be exaggerated). Even more than Toulouse, these Oriental mercantile cities represent an aborted urbanism that only momentarily achieves the autonomy and autocephaly known in Europe.

Japanese Port Cities

Mercantile cities appeared in Japan during the fourteenth through sixteenth centuries as port cities engaged in local and international trade.[8] The decay of bureaucratic state government over these centuries had reduced Japan to a multitude of warring feudal magnates whose dominions and powers were highly localized. Mercantile cities grew up in the interstices of this decentralized state society, and they persisted until the Tokugawa period discussed in the previous chapter again returned bureaucratic state control to Japan. During their brief ascendancy, cities such as Sakai (called the Venice of Japan), Nara, and Amagasaki reenacted many of the developments that their counterparts in medieval Europe witnessed.

Sakai was the most politically autonomous and economically independent of these Japanese port centers. Its commerce rested on textiles, lacquer ware, metal castings, rice, lumber, and salt. The city was a site for

---

[8]Cf. Takeo Yazaki, *Social Change and the City in Japan: From Earliest Times Through the Industrial Revolution*, trans. by David L. Swain (Japan Publications, Inc., 1968).

periodic markets and import warehouses, and its resident population consisted of wholesalers, transporters, and exchange brokers. This wealthy commercial elite—the equivalent of the medieval patriciate—controlled Sakai and other Japanese port cities, and staffed the administrative councils that formed their municipal governments.

Yet the political and economic independence of these Japanese mercantile cities was always tenuous. They depended heavily for commercial capital on monied feudal lords or rich religious foundations. Their major guarantee of political independence was the extent to which powerful feudal lords were so engaged in mutual annihilation that the ports were left untouched. Sakai and other cities also paid large bribes to such threatening rural magnates. By the sixteenth century, Japanese mercantile cities were doomed in spite of the defensive measures—moats, weapon stockpiles, and mercenary soldiers—that some of them took to guarantee their urban freedom. At the beginning of the Tokugawa period, Sakai and other ports were absorbed into the expanding bureaucratic state. Their commercial wealth, political autonomy, and urban existence were extinguished or greatly reduced. Future urban development in Japan passed out of the mercantile context into the form of the castle town directly subsidized and supervised by central state authority. Not only did Japanese mercantile cities fail to achieve city-state existence, they never even gained a long-lasting partial autonomy from external state powers.

Javanese Bazar Towns

Another instance of the partial and shortlived emergence of mercantile cities comes from Java, where beginning in the fourteenth and fifteenth centuries port cities became independent political and economic centers. Clifford Geertz has contrasted Javanese inland "castle towns" of the river valleys (which correspond to regal-ritual or administrative cities) with the bazar towns of the northern coast that represent a mercantile urban type.[9] The inland castle towns acted as the political capitals of state dependent on peasant rice cultivation and served as the residences of the king, his courtiers, and the artisans and religious specialists who attended to royal wants. These castle towns also controlled coastal urban enclaves that contained traders from throughout southern and eastern Asia. Such bazar towns depended on international commerce rather than peasant rice and rested on an altogether different organizational and ideological base from the inland capitals. They were

[9]Clifford Geertz, "The Development of the Javanese Economy: A Socio-Cultural Approach" (Cambridge, Massachusetts: Center for International Studies, M.I.T., mimeo, 1956), p. 57.

"oriented toward the sea, toward movement rather than stability, toward cosmopolitanism rather than isolationism."[10]

As the power of the inland Javanese states waned in the centuries before Dutch colonialism completely disrupted indigenous conditions, these bazar coastal towns became independent or semi-independent collections of foreign merchants. Each town nominally was ruled by a local lord of the city who inhabited a walled capital, which was surrounded by extramural urban wards. Each ward was inhabited by a different ethnic group engaged in trade, and each was represented by a captain or merchant prince chosen from the ethnic group. No legal autonomy existed for the merchant elements. However, the relations of the ethnically segregated traders and their merchant princes to the local regent were very different from the inland relationship of peasant to king. Local rulers in the bazar towns relied heavily on commerce for their prosperity—a commerce that was in the hands of foreign traders represented by these powerful captains. Not omnipotent, local lords dealt with their merchant urban population as "merchant to merchant" rather than as king to subject. No urban community developed in Javanese bazar towns, and internal political self-determination was minimal. Nevertheless, these cities experienced a balance of power between merchant princes from various religious, racial, and national backgrounds. Such a balance of power made their political form much more representative than the castle towns of the interior. Wealth and therefore power were widely distributed in the city due to its reliance on international trade. Thus the local ruler could only hope to control efficiently rather than dominate completely the relatively independent and equal merchant captains within the urban location. Here again the achievement of mercantile urbanism is only partial. However, even this limited and short-lived occurrence in the Orient indicates that mercantile cities developed in the preindustrial world wherever state decentralization or decay combined with the emergence of sources of wealth within the city.

URBAN ADAPTATION
AND ORGANIZATION

What then is the adaptation of mercantile cities to the state societies in which they are set? For mercantile cities that became fully developed city-states the answer is simple: The organization and ideology of the city

[10]Geertz, "The Development of the Javanese Economy," p. 61.

were also the constituents of the state society. When the city was only an autonomous urban community within a larger state, however, the answer is more complex. Although the surrounding state society may have been either a weakly centralized variant of the bureaucratic type discussed in Chapter Four or a strong variety of the segmentary state analyzed in Chapter Three, the enclaved mercantile city operated like a private domain. The city had its own political integrity, citizen militias, economic procedures, craft associations, commercial monopolies, status system, and legal code. Whether city-state or autonomous urban community, therefore, mercantile cities were sharply defined from the surrounding society—either by having formed the center of the state or by having been urban enclaves within a political and economic order to which the city was foreign. Since the city-state was latent in all mercantile cities, the nature of the state society to which mercantile cities adapted was a reflection of the city itself. This was reflected in either the clear image of the city-state or the clouded one of the autonomous urban community.

The city-state and the state within the state—the two guises of the mercantile city—shared many common institutions that differentiated them from segmentary or bureaucratic states. Perhaps the most significant is the importance of acquired wealth over hereditary status in access to power. In all autonomous mercantile cities and city-states the rule of money was all powerful, and sufficient wealth could eventually eradicate the social disabilities of lowly birth. Mercantile cities characteristically experienced a constant shifting of social status, prestige, and political influence from some individuals or families to others as fortunes were made and lost. The established wealthy may have attempted to limit new claimants to superior status or to absorb them through marriage. Nevertheless, the mercantile urban pattern provides no natural way (as opposed to artificial means, such as legal exclusion of the newly rich) to limit the accumulation of wealth and its attendant assertion of higher status.

Within the city, therefore, the presence of wealth beyond the control of an external state elite meant that power and position became nonascriptive and that leadership and control developed within the local urban context. Mercantile cities had ruling groups, but these tended to be plutocracies rather than aristocracies of birth. The status hierarchy found in mercantile cities accentuated urban citizens (especially the notables, or patricians) with power and wealth from within the city rather than the appointees of a king or ruler. Such leading elements in these cities were at times rural powerholders who were absorbed into the urban sphere and intermixed with the urban notables whose wealth flowed from commerce. In other cases, the urban leadership was composed solely of wealthy traders or capitalists, and rural magnates were legally and sometimes forcibly excluded from the city. Whether an amalgam of people whose wealth flowed from landownership or from commerce, the notables of mercantile cities operated in a new social order where social mobility was open and where birth and heredity were not the main requirements for high social status and great political influence.

Great social mobility based on wealth accounted for the intense political factionalism typifying city-states and autonomous mercantile cities. Court intrigues or palace revolts in bureaucratic states attempted to seat a new claimant in an ascriptively-defined position as the king, prince, or emperor of the state. No such ascriptive surety attended political power in mercantile cities. Instead a constant struggle for precedence occurred in which contestants built up loyal followings from their own or lower status segments of the urban population. The Ciompi uprising in medieval Florence was partially engendered by conflict within patrician ranks. That conflict fed upon the misfortunes of urban laborers and the discontent of weaving contractors to create a major threat to the entire community. Toulouse and Padua also experienced endemic factionalism within the patrician class, again a symptom of the absence of ascriptively defined power positions within the city.

In a political system that lacks ascriptive offices and an economic regimen where constant changes in fortune are common, electoral institutions help determine both who is to serve in office and who is to decide political contests. Although universal adult suffrage was unknown in mercantile cities and city-states, dispersion of wealth and power introduced a representative quality to their governments. Padua and Florence as city-states and Toulouse as an autonomous urban community extended their franchises to a wider segment of the urban and state population than ever characterized segmentary or bureaucratic polities. Citizenship as a social and political status within the urban area conveyed powers on the individual equivalent to the hereditary prerogatives of an aristocracy or ruling elite. Attainment of citizenship was always difficult precisely because of the benefits and freedom it conferred on the individual. Although citizenship could be obtained through money payments, apprenticeship, or guild membership in medieval Padua and Florence, the most common way was through birth as the son of a citizen. Citizenship in mercantile cities thus took on the hereditary quality of an ascriptive status, one of the few techniques by which the ruling notables limited urban social mobility.

The realities of power and wealth in mercantile cities meant that the opinion of some citizens counted much more heavily than the suggestions of others. Even more, the great majority of the urban population—not only women and children, but also laborers, poor craftsmen, and others of the urban underprivileged—never achieved citizen status and was completely disfranchised. Yet in most mercantile cities, a steady percolation of political weight drew power downward from a small patrician elite to a large urban mass. This dispersion of power went further in some cities than others, yet the fact of popular uprisings was ever present and symptomatic of what the electoral system, the shifting economies, and the nonascriptive political systems permitted, although grudgingly.

The factional contests, the electoral systems, and the popular militias of mercantile cities all suggest how small and introverted these political entities were. Even as city-states, their territorial limits were closely set; numerous localized state societies characterize the mercantile urban pattern. The constitution of autonomous urban communities or city-states was not readily expandable territorially nor was it easy to project over an ever-widening urban population. Mercantile urban growth commonly depended on colonists (willing settlers of new commercial frontiers or recalcitrant exiles of factional politics) sent from a mother city to establish independent urban replicas in new regions.

Political fragmentation is characteristic in the city-state and mercantile urban pattern, as are the jealousy and fear of the outside that accompany such insularity. Perhaps that explains why they so often fell under the rule of signoria, or despotism, as a bitter antidote to their internal dissension and external paranoia. Each city and city-state was an island in a sea of others that it distrusted, a closed universe zealously protecting its commercial prerogatives and defending its political independence. At times mercantile cities opportunistically entered into military, political, or commercial confederations to achieve ends in common that they could not obtain separately. The Hansa confederation of medieval European cities in the Baltic trade is an example of commercial cooperation; the various Guelph and Ghibbeline alliances of the Italian cities represent political and military coordination. These confederations were a coming together of equals, a combination of many small, sharply bound, and aggressively independent urban communities wherein none lost their identity or retained membership once their individual advantage had been served.

URBAN IDEOLOGY

Provincialism and civic pride determine the ideology of the city and its ideological ties to the wider society. These ties were generally hostile in situations where the city stood as a bastion of commercial entre-

preneurship, social mobility, and artistic enlightenment against a more
conservative state ruling elite. However, in a fully-developed city-state,
the entire region was transformed according to urban ideas. The ideology of the city—of commercial profit, bourgeois life-styles, and achieved
status—flowed outward, and the countryside was bound by sentiment
and allegiance to the urban zones. In either case, the city is the center—
of affection or distaste; its very way of life signals what is most to be
admired or to be disowned for the larger society. The city becomes a
recognizable entity in terms of ideology and effect, the ideological com-
plement to the organization of the city as an urban community. In
mercantile cities, the urban way of life that was emulated or disowned
did not arise simply from the extravagance and luxury of the state elite
that resided in the city. The urban life-style is a function of the very
commercial and political organization of the city—an organization that
accentuates wealth over birth, usury and investment over feudal service
and dues, popular assembly and association over kin federations or
groups based on ascriptive ties. At times the larger society and its
political powers reacted violently against the mercantile city's way and
suppressed it; at other times, the mercantile city was victorious and
transformed the larger society to fit its own ideological dictates.

The ideology of mercantile cities, exemplified in the Florentine
and Paduan city-states, often contained an internal conflict between
novel commercial and social values that were urban and traditional
beliefs that were rural. The commercial wealth, social mobility, and
popular government of Padua and Florence both elicited and embodied
a changing world of ideology and religious values, works of art and
philosophy, and other manifestations of new values that entered medieval Italian society from its mercantile cities. Although the appearance of
politically autonomous cities in northern Italy preceded the full flower-
ing of the Renaissance, many of the latter period's characteristics were
presaged in medieval times. A sense of the city as the center of life and
loyalty to the urban community was a characteristic quality of the Italian cities. One Florentine wrote that his city was more important than his
children, a statement that was perhaps an exaggeration of the attach-
ment of the urban citizen to his home.[11] Yet this allegiance and loyalty to
the urban center as a community lay behind the subsidy of art and
architecture by the urban rich as well as their militant defense of urban
freedoms.

The increasing dominance of the rule of wealth over the prerogatives of birth in mercantile cities gave rise to a purely (mercantile) urban
code of behavior that is often typified as "bourgeois." The new social

[11]Brucker, *Renaissance Florence*, p. 139.

mobility that brought popular groups to power also allowed their entry into literature and philosophy, where they injected new interests and viewpoints. In Padua, the early humanists who turned toward the classical world for models and styles were self-made men, newly risen to the ranks of justices and notaries in the city. They attempted to define a role for the urban socially mobile. At times they reverted to the medieval notions of the noble and chivalrous, but they also looked for precedents in the classical world and its urban culture with which to instruct and rationalize the new world of their city.[12]

Yet the values and attitudes of the medieval world continued in strength, and there was constant dialogue between the older virtues of the Middle Ages and the new ones of the evolving mercantile centers. This interplay mirrored in the world of thought the give-and-take between urban commune and rural aristocrat that characterized the political process. The values of the bourgeois urbanites contrasted with noble violence, chivalry, and contempt for trade. The medieval ideals of corporation and association rather than individualism became embodied in the patrician families and guilds. Such ideals dictated the overwhelming relevance of family and patron-client relations in the forging of political factions, economic commercial connections, and military units. The religious proscription of usury—interest-bearing loans necessary to any expanding economy—is another relic of a former world that continued and troubled the enterprising citizens of medieval Italian cities. In Padua, this ambivalence was more evident than in Florence: Moneylenders were looked down on, yet social opprobrium alone could not prevent their sons from advancing to the influential and elevated social statuses that their wealth, however ill-gotten, permitted. It has been suggested that in Florence the artistic and architectural outpourings of the city were funded from the religious guilt of the merchants.[13] Whatever the ultimate psychological reason, the citizenry—through their guilds, their religious associations, their civic government—created an urban plan that embodied both their commercial wealth and their own perspective on the city.

The mercantile cities and city-states discussed in this chapter represent an urban type that develops under weak state rule and urban economic autonomy. These cities were centers of innovation in commerce, government, and social stratification within the state societies into which they were set. Mercantile cities commonly conflicted with pre-

[12]Hyde, *Padua in the Age of Dante*, pp. 121–153.
[13]Brucker, *Renaissance Florence*, p. 108.

existing state societies. In the ensuing contest, the urban locale may have lost and been absorbed under state control, may have compromised and gained a fragile autonomy within state jurisdiction, or may have won and developed into a city-state that impressed its organization and ideology onto the wider society.

The mercantile city is the final preindustrial type of primary urbanism demarcated in this book. Our survey of preindustrial urban types—regal-ritual cities, administrative cities, and mercantile cities—has traveled in a diachronic perspective to cities as geographically removed as those in Japan and Europe and as temporally distant as the twentieth-century Swazi and the ninth-century Carolingian realm. The following chapters concern the primary urban types that appear after the advent of Western industrialism. We view them through a diachronic perspective that charts the developmental pattern of individual cities.

6

Colonial Cities

Many state societies of Asia, Africa, and the New World were until recently the colonial dependencies of Western industrial nations. Their acquisition of independence over the last several decades has not effaced the legacy of colonialism from their societies or cities. The many problems that beset these societies as they attempt to industrialize—overpopulation, insufficient agricultural production, political dissension—have their analogs in urban locales. Overurbanization and slums filled with urban villagers, disruption of traditional urban organization, and the rise of a new political competition for wealth and power are among the cities' problems. These unique characteristics of such state societies are often developments from their colonial past. Subject to Western political and/or economic domination, such societies and their cities were partly transformed to fit industrial patterns. New power was given the state and new cities were built (or old ones reconstituted) by the colonial masters. The dominated society, its peasant population, and its urban dwellers were linked to the Western industrial nation (France, Britain, Italy, and others) so as to maximize the economic and political profits while minimizing the costs of colonial rule. This domination therefore brought many societies in Asia, Africa, and the Americas within the industrial world without allowing them full attainment of industrial economic and political institutions. Now independent, these former colonial dependencies suffer from a peculiar "half-way" condition: They are no longer preindustrial and not yet industrial. Political, economic, and urban problems that ensue from this transition still are not solved (and perhaps never will be). This chapter details the anomalous quality of such state societies and the colonial primary urban type associated with them.

The typology of primary urbanism associates such colonial cities with highly bureaucratic states wherein the urban area is not an autonomous economic center for the production of industrial wealth. Instead, the state society and its cities depend heavily on peasant subsistence agriculture to feed the urban population and subsidize state government. Unlike industrial cities, then, the cultural role of the colonial urban type depends on administrative functions such as were performed by administrative cities. But the colonial city enveloped in an industrial world is different from the administrative city of the preindustrial. Colonial domination by industrial powers acted to centralize, sophisticate, and bureaucratize state control and the urban elites who exercised it far beyond what was possible in preindustrial bureaucratic states and administrative cities. This great concentration of power is in part a result of the foreign and basically exploitative colonial rule that Western industrial nations introduced. More importantly, the industrial technology developed in their home countries permitted the colonial masters of Asian, African, and New World societies to intervene and control their colonies as never before possible. Railroads, telegraphs, repeating rifles, metalled roads, artillery, and later, automobiles, radios, airplanes, machine guns, and propaganda films exemplify the industrial technology used to buttress this powerful state apparatus.

The ideology of rule was also often transformed by Western industrial models. Democratic elections, party politics, legislatures, presidents or prime ministers, and an electorate composed of all adults became the standard in many newly independent colonies. Scions taken from an industrial society and poorly grafted onto a colonial one, these institutions all too quickly withered in many places. Some, however, did sprout and grow to define the ideology of government espoused in many new nations: the welfare state responsible for economic development and a social policy that ameliorates inequities and enhances life; the competition for political power outside ascribed statuses based on kinship, caste, pedigree or faith; the nation as a homogeneous cultural sphere inspiring the allegiance of its citizens.

Colonial powers generally did not pursue equivalent industrial innovations in the economic sphere. For their greater economic benefit and political mastery (as we will see below), they fossilized the productivity of their colonies at a preindustrial level. Rural subsistence agriculture—rather than urban factories and rural agro-businesses—remained the major economic resources; when the latter existed their profits went to the home country instead of the colonized population. This anomalous combination of an industrial political order with a preindustrial peasant economy characterizes former colonial dependencies and defines the nature of these state societies.

PRISMATIC STATE
AND COLONIAL CITY

Like an astronaut in full space gear astride a donkey, such state societies in many newly independent nations of Asia, Africa, and the Americas have perplexed scholars because they are novel and aberrant combinations of preindustrial and industrial elements. A decade ago these societies were commonly perceived as "transitional" between the polar types of "traditional" and "modern." That is, they were presumed to be in the process of changing from social orders where men of different birth, caste, tribe, or religion legitimately claimed different levels of power and wealth (and women usually did not count at all) to societies where all persons were in theory equal before the law and in the pursuit of opportunity. But as their economic development snail-paced along, as their formal democratic governments increasingly became the tools of military or despotic rule, and as their social problems multiplied, the supposed transitional character of these societies assumed a stability and permanency that belied rapid change. These new nations evidently possessed political, economic, and social institutions that were not simply the logical steps in a straight-line development from preindustrial to industrial forms.

Neither traditional nor modern, these state societies, according to Fred Riggs, are "prismatic" in that they combine preindustrial and industrial institutions and refract them into new social forms.[1] Because they are mixtures and reformulations of the preindustrial and the industrial, prismatic state societies may appear as innovative versions of preindustrial states but at the same time look like aberrant copies of industrial societies. Many of their governmental and political characteristics would

[1]Fred W. Riggs, *Administration in Developing Countries: The Theory of Prismatic Society* (Boston: Houghton Mifflin Company, 1964).

be labelled "corruptions" or "breakdowns in the system" if (or when) they occurred in our own society. Thus a typical prismatic pattern is for state power to be organized within a highly elaborate administration. This administration bureaucratizes government throughout the society by the uniform standards that we assume must exist in any modern, industrial country. But outside the capital and the main governmental bureaus located there, in backwater regions or rural villages, the formal administration of the prismatic state dissolves or fades away. Instead of being ruled by government agency and bureaucrat, these areas are governed by the local village council, tribal ruler, caste pancayat, or other ascriptive, preindustrial, and local institutions. Or if the formal administrative organization does operate, it is because a traditional leader or council functions in the old ways with new titles: Chiefs become bureaucrats; caste councils become village committees. Whatever their new bureaucratic titles, such persons and institutions regulate social life through traditional influence and authority rather than through the power invested in their new offices by state rulers. The elaborate bureaucratic structure based on industrial models may thus be "hollow" in many spheres of a prismatic state society.[2]

Another characteristic of prismatic states is an extreme competition for political office or administrative position, a competition unhindered by either traditional values or (industrial) egalitarian selection methods. In the colonial pasts of most prismatic societies, bureaucratic positions were the main roads to wealth and influence open to the native population. Like the Mamluks in their administrative cities, the British, French, German, or other colonial powers could not rule without a local cadre of government officials who were loyal and adept at administration. The colonial rulers limited the power and prestige attached to all institutions other than the political institutions through which they governed the colony. Education, commerce, and wealth were not ends in themselves for the aspiring South Asian, African, or Latin American because they could only lead to preferment and social mobility when they were used to gain government positions. After independence and the creation of at least formal democracy, another avenue of success was added to the purely administrative realm: the pursuit of seats in legislatures, cabinets, parliaments, and other presumably popularly elected bodies. But the rules by which this competition is carried forward in prismatic states are based on neither ascription nor egalitarian access. Individuals partly freed from the restraints of family, caste, and community use guile, violence, bribery, and nepotism (where family connections are activated

[2]*Ibid.*, pp. 13–14.

for individual ends) to achieve their goals. Political parties and ideologies based on industrial models often only mask the individual's pursuit of wealth and power in the political sphere. Concomitantly, politics and administration are not separated, because individuals use political leverage to achieve bureaucratic posts. Similarly, bureaucrats engage in political activities to reinforce their positions or enlarge their personal gain.[3] When such activities occur in industrial states they are condemned and sometimes even punished; in prismatic states they represent accepted strategies for those who seek a privileged position.

However, ascriptively-defined groups also compete in the formal political machinery, and their presence indicates how inadequately the ideal model of industrial state organization fits the new nations. Communal or religious political parties, caste or tribal associations, and other partly ascriptive and partly voluntary organizations (in that members choose to join but must be of specific kin groups, religions, tribes, or castes) seek privileges and concessions for their own constituents within the political-bureaucratic system. Electorates or pressure groups thus form around traditional institutions, which are thereby altered to further their success in the political arena.[4]

The prismatic state is thus a highly bureaucratic state based on an industrial model that is continually compromised in operation. Personal ambition that recognizes no moral limits, communal loyalties that interweave an ascriptive element, and local level preindustrial institutions and leadership that abrogate the formal administrative chain all indicate the refraction characteristic of prismatic states.

Why do preindustrial institutions and identities exist and compromise the formal bureaucratic system introduced under former colonial masters? Why does an unrestrained personal ambition corrupt the reconstruction of politics and administration along the lines of industrial states? To answer these questions, we must look at how colonial rule fossilized the economic productivity of these prismatic states, how it preserved traditional social relationships and groups while partially altering them in such a way that they were no longer preindustrial but not yet industrial. This process, which Clifford Geertz has called "agricultural involution" in Java,[5] characterizes many of the former colonies controlled by Western industrial nations. It represents the major way in which these industrial states economically exploited and politically subdued their colonial dependencies.

---

[3] *Ibid.*, p. 262.

[4] Riggs refers to such partially-ascriptive groups as clects. *Ibid.*, pp. 169–73.

[5] Clifford Geertz, *Agricultural Involution: The Process of Ecological Change in Indonesia* (Berkeley: University of California Press, 1968).

Javanese Agricultural Involution

When the Dutch became colonial masters of Java, they inherited a preindustrial bureaucratic state dependent on intensive rice cultivation by a rural peasantry.[6] As in most colonial situations where the native population is left on the land, the primary objective of the Dutch was to extract the maximum economic profit from Java at minimal administrative cost. At the time of conquest, the Javanese peasant's life was defined by the rice field he worked, by his family and kinsmen, by the village community in which he lived, and by the rituals and religious observances appropriate to each of these daily spheres. Had the Dutch introduced an industrial economy in Java, the peasant's limited subsistence and social requirements might have been transformed into the unlimited consumption desires and the (more or less developed) political activism of the factory worker or farm laborer in industrial Europe. Yet the Dutch were not simply content to extract a large proportion of the peasants' rice production, as had the former rulers. The rice produced beyond the peasants' subsistence needs was not of sufficient quantity or of high enough market value to create the economic capital that Dutch colonialism needed to fuel the industrial economy of the homeland.

How then to introduce cash crops with high value in international markets into a peasant subsistence economy? How, that is, without transforming the peasant into an industrial worker or rural proletarian with potentially greater consumption and political demands? The Culture System introduced by the Dutch in 1830 was an ingenious solution to this dilemma. It was a solution, however, that originated the prismatic conditions that have plagued Java (and Indonesia) up to the present day. Under the Culture System, each Javanese peasant was forced to grow sugar cane on two-fifths of his land and turn the harvested crop over to the government as taxes. Since the agricultural requirements of sugar cane were similar to those for irrigated rice, the peasant need not alter his traditional methods or relationship to the land even though he produced a nonsubsistence crop destined for the international market. Since the peasant was not involved in the marketing of this crop, he was not introduced into an industrial cash economy. The Culture System thus effectively fused preindustrial and industrial patterns in such a way that the one did not fully replace the other; rather both combined in an

[6]The following materials on Java are taken from Clifford Geertz, *The Social History of an Indonesian Town* (Cambridge, Massachusetts: The M.I.T. Press, 1965).

amalgam that was anomalous and yet stable. The peasant reaped the crop; the Dutch reaped the profits and exported them to the home country. The industrial economy of the Netherlands was augmented; the Javanese peasant remained constrained within a preindustrial economy and society that were rapidly becoming prismatic.

At the end of the nineteenth century, the Culture System gave way to a plantation economy in private (Dutch) hands. These plantations continued a modified form of the Culture System by renting peasant rice land for the production of sugar cane. But the plantations also utilized previously vacant land in the cultivation of coffee, cassava, tea, and sisal. They employed seasonal wage laborers drawn from the peasantry to work on this land and in the mills that processed sugar cane. Plantations invested capital in larger land holding peasants to secure a more reliable crop and more experienced cultivators. Thus the rise of plantations began to convert smaller land holding peasants into wage laborers—a rural proletariat—while making the larger landholders into agricultural capitalists—farmers as we know them. These developments promised to transform the peasantry and the local economy along modern industrial lines wholly unlike the Culture System.

The world-wide depression of the 1930s sent sugar prices plummeting and put an abrupt end to this transformation of peasant agriculture and Javanese society. Geertz suggests that even had this economic calamity not occurred, the full transformation would have proved difficult to accomplish. Like the Culture System before it, the plantation economy restrained the impact of capitalist and industrial organization on the Javanese peasantry. Wages were kept low and employment was seasonal, so that the peasant could not become a full-time wage laborer. Mobility up through the ranks to high positions in the plantation directorate was virtually impossible, and this too kept the Javanese in his village and on his land. Crops other than sugar cane, whose cultivation could not be undertaken by the peasantry without great change in agricultural timing and technology, were grown on nonpeasant lands directly controlled by the plantations. The result, as Geertz aptly suggests, was "Western capitalist enterprise with Eastern precapitalist land and labor, the latter largely enclosed in a traditional structure."[7]

The Great Depression, the ensuing war years, and the post-war struggle against Dutch colonialism reinforced this condition. After independence, when the Japanese and Dutch had been thrust out and the plantation economy much reduced, Java still contended with a peasant economy transformed but fossilized by a century of colonial rule. A

[7] *Ibid.*, p. 46.

prismatic state society held sway as an obvious outcome of and response to this dilemma.

Land and Market in British India

From the second half of the eighteenth through the middle of the nineteenth centuries, the British East India Company increasingly threw off its original commercial orientation to become the premier political power on the Indian subcontinent. As it conquered or was ceded new lands and the peasantry upon them, "John Company" grew more and more involved in the management of rural land tenure in order to insure its economic gain and preserve its political control over India. Land tenures and the Company's administration of them varied in different parts of the subcontinent. The following material from North India is one example of how Company rule initially altered peasant tenures sufficiently to overturn the traditional system, and then subsequently muted the capitalist impact of these early policies. In northern India, the British created a prismatic condition similar to the Javanese, but one arising through a different colonial policy.

When the British gained control over much of the present state of Uttar Pradesh (formerly called the United Provinces), their first task was to establish who owned the land and therefore who was responsible for paying the land revenue upon which Company finances heavily depended.[8] Implicit in British notions was an industrial capitalist model where land, like all property, could be bought, sold, and leased at market-determined prices by a proprietor. The indigenous preindustrial model was very different from such European notions. Rather than a single proprietor, many individuals "owned" a specific piece of land in northern India in the sense that they all had certain customary privileges in its use and the enjoyment of its agricultural product. A wide range of social classes—from the peasant who actually tilled the field to the raja who collected the land revenue from it—exercised such usufructary rights. But no one owned the land in the sense of a capital resource that could be bought, sold, rented, or in other ways disposed of for profit. Under preindustrial conditions in India, no market in land existed to set capitalist prices on this commodity: The peasant paid customary, not market-determined, revenue or rental rates; the raja or local overlord col-

<hr/>

[8]This discussion of North Indian land tenure and British colonial policy follows Walter C. Neale, *Economic Change in Rural India: Land Tenure and Reform in Uttar Pradesh, 1800–1955* (New Haven: Yale University Press, 1962).

lected a customary proportion of the peasant's harvest, in either kind or cash.

Because they could not condone or would not conceive of a land tenure pattern in which no capitalist proprietor existed, the British quickly invested individuals or groups with full property rights based on European notions. They ignored the fact that usufructary rights in land subsumed a wide social spectrum—overlord and peasant follower, corporate village brotherhoods, village headman and village service castes—and arbitrarily invested some of them with proprietorship while dispossessing the others of the land privileges they had traditionally enjoyed. They disregarded the fact that land had no market-determined price under the traditional system and introduced land auctions when the "owners" they appointed defaulted on their onerous revenue payments. They overlooked the fact that tenant cultivators did not pay market rental rates, and left their futures to the untender mercies of the newly created landlords who now could evict them or increase their rentals with little concern for custom. The East India Company policy set in motion a proprietary upheaval that at great social cost created a capitalist market in land and a class of indigenous landowners willing to profit from this new market. John Company's actions were the prelude to an industrial reorganization of North Indian land and agriculture.

But like the Javanese plantation economy, the Indian rural economy was transformed only so much. By the latter nineteenth and early twentieth centuries, it came to a standstill halfway between preindustrial and industrial forms. As had the Dutch, the British feared that the proprietary transformation that they had set in motion might have adverse effects on the political stability of their South Asian colony. At this point too, the British did not depend so heavily for government finance on maximizing their land revenue; the profit-making East India Company had been replaced by the British Crown as rulers of India. The fossilization of the rural economy was accomplished by a series of regulations that limited the impact of the new capitalism in land. These restrictions took two forms.

Tenancy legislation effectively restricted the proprietor's freedom to obtain the highest market rental for his land. By conferring occupancy rights on tenants who possessed their lands for a specified number of years, the British government disallowed evictions by the proprietor and thus his pursuit of higher profits. Other legislation limited the proprietor's freedom to increase rents. The colonial administration thus became the arbiter of "fair" (clearly an anti-capitalist sentiment) land rental rates. The impersonal capitalist market for land and tenancy that was in the process of formation was summarily sent packing by the arbitrary power of British colonial government—the same power that had invited it to northern India in the first place.

The British also restricted the impact of market forces on the proprietors. They enacted legislation that limited the owner's right to sell his land and controlled the amount of debt and the rate of interest he could carry. This legislation, although it protected the property owner, also acted to restrict the market in land, to cushion the peasant economy from capitalist and modernizing forces. It created a rural economy in which modified preindustrial elements intermixed with industrial capitalist ones. Together they engendered a prismatic condition that continues to plague and hinder rural economic development in independent India.

URBAN ADAPTATION AND ORGANIZATION

The prismatic condition of the wider state society calls forth two very different and seemingly contradictory adaptations in the colonial city. Their contradictory character is just another instance of the uneasy but stable social amalgam that the prismatic society represents.

One urban adaptation concerns the very rapid growth of cities in prismatic states through peasant migration from the countryside. Whether pulled to the city and its amenities by new values introduced under colonial rule or pushed out of the rural area by a stagnant economy (equally a legacy of former domination), peasants in Asia and Latin America have swarmed into urban locales over the last half-century. However, this rapid urbanization leads to consequences in colonial cities very different from those that characterized nineteenth-century industrial urbanization in the West. Because the colonial city is not economically autonomous, because it is not the center of an expanding industrial economy, rapid urbanization does not lead to the absorption of the rural migrants into an industrial way of life. They are urban in residence but rural in the lives they lead and the ideas they hold. They usually occupy the lowest rungs in the urban labor market; they often inhabit the most decrepit and crowded sections of the city—sometimes even marking off their living quarters and carrying out domestic arrangements on the streets themselves. Their poor wages are commonly used to satisfy only the most minimal standards of existence so they can free more money for remittances to their rural homes. Their residential segregation, their rural speech and habits, and their impoverished condition earn such migrants the derision of other urbanites. Yet the migrants must also bear the opprobrium of their rural origins, because the colonial city offers little opportunity for their full integration into the urban sphere. This urban adaptation is clearly a response to the lack of industrial expansion in the colonial city and the lack of economic transformation in the rural areas of the prismatic state society.

The other urban adaptation occurs among the core population of the city who control its political and economic life. This adaptation has been most clearly recognized by anthropologists in the small towns of prismatic state societies, but it undoubtedly occurs as well in the large colonial cities that have taken the brunt of rural migration. The urban core population evidences an adaptation to the political-bureaucratic apparatus of the prismatic state society. The old links between preindustrial city and bureaucratic state (links that were based on an urban hierarchy of administrative duties) are set aside for a more open and competitive interaction. Family, kin, religious, and other communal and ascriptive associations intermix with individuals pursuing their own gain, and they compete for power and wealth in the urban political arena. Local urban factions, many of a traditional character, link up with national parties and ideologies. The ostensibly democratic forms and the supposedly rational bureaucratic machinery of the prismatic state are redefined and manipulated in the urban context. They are used to solve kin and family conflicts, competitions between castes or other communal groups, or animosity between religious faiths. It is a competition where all are presumably equal and he who has the most votes wins. But these votes are gathered through appeals to ascriptive identity or by recourse to bribery, nepotism, and bureaucratic patronage. The political-bureaucratic system patterned after Western industrial nations is refracted by traditional associations and groups. Thus a wholly new political arena for conflict and competition is created.

The urban core adapts and alters the organization of the city to fit the realities of political power and office in the prismatic state. The urban migrants, on the other hand, are never fully absorbed into the urban sphere; they retain traditional ways as insulation and protection from the city populace, which both exploits and disowns them. The urban core adaptation leads to the penetration of the city by new political parties and ideologies—mere covers for communal or individual ambition though they may be. The urban migrant adaptation leads to an insularity from the city and a removal from this political competition. Urban migrants are thus removed from the process that generates the new links between colonial city and prismatic society. If not in the exact duplication of rural ways, then at least in this isolation from the urban core, these recent migrants appear as villagers in cities. The following cases illustrate the two adaptations that characterize colonial cities and the migrant or core populations that inhabit them.

Urban Villagers

The theme of "overurbanization" is current in the study of new nations. This concept refers to the very rapid growth of colonial cities through migration from the rural countryside and the simultaneous failure of such cities to absorb their mushrooming populations into industrial employment.[9] Overurbanization in colonial cities means that large segments of the city's population suffer extreme poverty, misery, and a substandard life-style. The squalor of Bombay, the overcrowding of Calcutta, the "slumscrapers" for the poor in Rio, and similar conditions in other colonial cities are notorious examples of the physical deprivation and breakdown of facilities associated with overurbanization. But there are social consequences as well. The migrant adapts to his lowly economic condition, his pejorative social status, his exclusion from mainstream urban life, by retaining many rural ways. These are readapted to the urban context to provide a supportive milieu for the migrant's difficult life in the city.

Whether about Mexico, Ethiopia, India, Peru, or Egypt,[10] most studies of recent migrants to colonial cities report a continued "ruralism" as characteristic of their social organization. Some traits identified as rural may have arisen among migrants as adaptations to the colonial city whether or not they existed in their natal villages. The urban life-style of North Indian migrants to the city of Bombay provides a good example of ruralism. William Rowe found that these migrants work as itinerant hawkers, small shopkeepers, public transport operators, and in other unskilled or semi-skilled jobs that pay poorly and confer little status. The very name by which North Indian migrants are known in Bombay—*bhaiya*—is abusive and a reference to their rustic speech (bhaiya means

[9]Cf. Daniel Lerner, "Comparative Analysis of Processes of Modernisation," in *The City in Modern Africa*, Horace Miner, ed. (London: Pall Mall Press, 1967).
[10]Lewis, "Urbanization Without Breakdown: A Case Study," *The Scientific Monthly*, LXXV, 1 (1952); W. A. Shack, "Urban Ethnicity and the Cultural Process of Urbanization in Ethiopia;" William L. Rowe, "Caste, Kinship, and Association in Urban India;" William Mangin, "Sociological, Cultural, and Political Characteristics of Some Urban Migrants in Peru," all in *Urban Anthropology: Cross-Cultural Studies of Urbanization*, Aidan Southall, ed. (New York: Oxford University Press, 1973). Also Mangin's articles collected in *Peasants in Cities: Readings in the Anthropology of Urbanization*, William Mangin, ed. (Boston: Houghton Mifflin, 1970) and Janet Abu-Lughod, "Migrant Adjustment to City Life: The Egyptian Case," *The American Journal of Sociology*, LXVII, 1 (1961).

"brother" but is used by migrants as a general form of address). The bhaiya's image of the city is often equally negative. He views his residence there as economically necessary but impermanent (even though he may spend most of his adult working life in Bombay). He adopts an urban life-style that is greatly restricted and inexpensive so that he can remit the maximum amount of his small earnings to close kinsmen (usually including his wife and children) in his home village.

Kinship and caste organize the residential ties of the bhaiyas and segregate them into enclaves within the city. Men of the same caste and home village or nearby villages form residential units in Bombay. These residential units provide later migrants with shelter, job information, and a sense of security. Real or fictive kin ties are an important social cement within these groups; and migrants therefore interact in terms of familiar village categories of caste, kinship, and region of origin rather than on the basis of class or occupational status. Each caste-kin residential unit has a leader, generally older and with more years of urban experience, who acts as a broker between the migrants and agencies of the city such as police, landlords, and employers. These leaders exert a conservative influence over their followers and help maintain appropriate village caste and ritual behaviors among them. Because these kin-caste residential units are so strong and surround the bhaiyas' social lives so completely, migrants have little contact with non-bhaiya urbanites, and they tend not to participate in the new political associations of the colonial city (which we will describe later for a North Indian town).

Detached by status, employment, residence, and attitude from the main currents of the city, the Bombay bhaiya uses traditional forms of kinship, caste, and belief to make his way in the city for limited economic purposes. In the process, he suffers scorn and poverty, and remains "at the far end of the continuum of involvement in city life."[11]

Oscar Lewis, in one of the first studies of overurbanization, found a similar ruralism among migrants in Mexico City. They too resided in neighborhood enclaves within the city (called *vecindades*), which "act as a shock absorber for the rural migrants to the city because of the similarity between its culture and that of rural communities."[12] Thus, family ties not only remained stable among the Mexican migrants, they were even strengthened and extended to more distant kin within the city. However, there was a tendency for more matrifocal families to appear in the urban context. Ritual co-parenthood (*compadrazgo*) and other village

---

[11]Rowe, "Caste, Kinship, and Association in Urban India," p. 232.

[12]Oscar Lewis, "Further Observations on the Folk-Urban Continuum and Urbanization with Special Reference to Mexico City," in *The Study of Urbanization*, Philip M. Hauser and Leo F. Schnore, eds. (New York: John Wiley & Sons, Inc., 1965).

customs and beliefs continued unabated, although religious practices conformed in even greater degree to Catholic ideals.

Some urban villagers eventually become absorbed into the city. In Peru and Brazil, for example, the most enterprising of them often break away from the inner-city slums to form shanty towns or "tin can cities" as squatters on public lands.[13] Through political pressure and the squatters' own initiative, urban facilities such as water, electricity, shops, and roads are introduced to the shanty town settlement. It eventually may become fully absorbed into the city, and its population may become fully urban in orientation. However, such developments are at best limited to a fraction of the urban migrants, and even then they are not always successful because police and urban authorities resist them with great force.

If the retention of rural life-ways by urban migrants is related to the lack of an industrial economy in the colonial city, then we should expect that urbanization in industrial cities would lead to much greater transformation in the migrant population (although, as the shanty town cases indicate, individual disposition is another important ingredient). The history of rapid acculturation of immigrant groups in the United States during the nineteenth and twentieth centuries is an example of such a migrant transformation. Within several generations after migration, the Irish, Germans, Italians, Jews, Greeks, and Poles altered language, values, family forms, and other life-ways in accord with the new industrial opportunities they met in American cities. Indeed, their very identification as "Italian" or "Polish" is an indication of how peasants from many different villages, regions, and dialect areas in the home country came to recognize a common ethnicity under the pressures of adaptation to industrial America.[14] Although such identities and the cuisines, religions, languages, and general customs that underlie them continue to characterize Italian-Americans as in some sense Italian, or American Jews as to some degree Jewish, the basic involvement of former immigrants in modern American institutions is unquestioned.

Another example of the type of urbanization that leads to the transformation rather than the retention of traditional life-ways comes from the literature on African migration to industrial mining cities or other urban places characterized by an industrial economy. Among these African migrants, the old tribal identities die and are replaced with new ethnic affiliations. Such ethnic affiliations merge many tribal groups

---

[13]Mangin, *Peasants in Cities*, p. 55; and Anthony Leeds, "The Significant Variables Determining the Character of Squatter Settlements," *America Latina* XII, 3 (1969).

[14]Cf. Herbert J. Gans, *The Urban Villagers: Group and Class in the Life of Italian-Americans* (New York: Free Press, 1962); Florian Znaniecki and William Isaac Thomas, *The Polish Peasant in Europe and America* (New York: Alfred A. Knopf, 1927).

into a single urban association or identity—a process similar to what happened among the European migrants to the United States.[15] Like ethnic associations in nineteenth-century American cities, they also organize many social benefits for their members: burial societies, credit unions, and other mutual aid associations and services not provided in the formal institutions of the industrial city.

Yet even in these African cities, urban villagers exist. For example, the Fulbe migrants to Lunsar in Sierre Leone do not fit the common pattern of urbanization in this mining city. Since these devout Muslims do not send their children to the local Christian schools, they cannot gain employment except in traditional activities such as cattle trading. The Fulbe therefore neither enter the industrial economy of the city nor break with village ways or village connections.[16] A similar condition exists among the Xhosa migrants to East London in South Africa. Some members of this tribe have chosen to remain illiterate and pagan and are never fully integrated into the urban locale. The others, who are educated and Christian, fully find their niche within the industrial city.[17] Under industrial urbanization then, some degree of choice is given to migrants to remain urban villagers or become full urbanites, just as in colonial cities some individuals have the initiative to break out of ruralism and form shanty towns.

The rural economy of the prismatic state in conjunction with the nonindustrial economy of the colonial city produces overurbanization and makes urban villagers out of recent migrants. We now turn to the effects of prismatic state society on the core population of the colonial city.

Colonial Town in Prismatic Society

Tezibazar is a town of about seven thousand people situated in the Gangetic plain of northern India, some fifty miles from Banaras.[18] Its history begins at an undetermined point in the past (approximately four hundred years ago) when the urban area was founded as a low-level

---

[15]Cf. J. Clyde Mitchell, *The Kalela Dance: Aspects of Social Relationships Among Urban Africans in Northern Rhodesia*, Rhodes-Livingstone Institute, Paper No. 27 (Manchester, England: University Press, 1956).

[16]Kenneth Lindsay Little, "Urbanization and Regional Associations: Their Paradoxical Function," in *Urban Anthropology: Cross-Cultural Studies of Urbanization*, Aidan Southall, ed. (New York: Oxford University Press, 1973).

[17]Little, "Urbanization and Regional Associations," pp. 409–10.

[18]A detailed description and analysis of Tezibazar is given in Richard G. Fox, *From Zamindar to Ballot Box: Community Change in a North Indian Market Town* (Ithaca, New York: Cornell University Press, 1969).

administrative center for a Muslim bureaucratic state. The first governor appointed by the Muslim conquerors, Havi Viyar Khan, constructed a fort, a mosque, and a market place in what is now the northern section of the town. Havi Viyar had been granted by the state rulers the right to collect land revenue from one thousand acres and the peasants thereon; and Tezibazar in its early years was, like all administrative cities, a locale from which the elite controlled the peasantry and collected their wealth. The newly constructed market place and the protection afforded commerce by the governor and his descendants attracted merchant castes (collectively known as *baniyas*) to the growing urban locale. The Khan family thus controlled not only the surrounding rural area but also the urban market and the population that grew up around it. They arbitrated disputes, enacted or enforced the laws, and formed the main links between Tezibazar and the bureaucratic state.

After the Indian Mutiny of 1857, that is about a half-century after British colonial rule had been instituted in this part of northern India, the fortunes of the Khan family began to decline. Under British rule, they lost any official position in the government of the town or rural area and were converted into large property owners by the process described earlier in this chapter. At the end of the nineteenth century, they were forced to sell their land to wealthy baniya families in the town, and in the early decades of the twentieth century their urban influence and wealth were dissipated by the wanton and riotous life-style of the family head.

While the Khan family moved toward financial disaster and poverty, a new urban development began in the southern part of present-day Tezibazar. Shortly after the 1857 Mutiny, a local raja named Udai Baks purchased this southern area and began to develop it as an administrative center from which to oversee his extensive rural property nearby. The raja constructed a large Hindu temple and an impressive mansion behind it; a short distance away he endowed an extensive market place, which subsequently became the main grain market in Tezibazar. Merchants soon flocked to the raja's urban settlement, just as they had earlier been led to the Khans' further north. By the end of the nineteenth century, two urban areas existed in what is now Tezibazar town, each formed under the aegis of local overlords in a fashion typical of administrative cities.

The urban authority held by Udai Baks and his successors was very similar to the urban influence exercised by the Khans. They guaranteed the "peace of the market" for merchants who feared the loss of money and even life in the rough and tumble of rural existence. They financed and supervised Hindu festivals in Tezibazar and undoubtedly acted as mediators in family, caste, or commercial disputes.

The power and influence of Udai Baks did not survive the beginning of the twentieth century. After the raja's death in 1899, his daughter continued to live in their impressive town house until her demise in 1916. Although she attempted to continue Udai Baks's authority in urban affairs, she was unsuccessful except in the organization of Hindu ritual festivals. Her death, which coincided with the impoverishment of the Khan family, meant that the traditional class of overlords passed from the Tezibazar scene.

In 1907 the British colonial government formed the single municipality of Tezibazar by joining the northern and southern urban developments. The new town was governed by a committee of British bureaucrats and urban residents, the latter chosen by the British from the overlord families of the town. Within ten years, however, the influence of this traditional elite was either extinguished or in eclipse, as we have seen. By the early 1920s, their involvement in urban affairs had passed to a few baniya families who had replaced their original commercial orientation with incomes derived from rural property. These baniya families gave alms to the poor, provided lodging for religious pilgrims, built temples, subsidized ritual performances, and mediated disputes between members of the urban population. But because they were less wealthy, their pedigrees less august, and their status and activities less institutionalized, the baniyas maintained the traditional overlordship of the town in only a very diminished way. At the end of World War II, the limited prestige and urban influence of these landowning baniyas were in eclipse. The war and the inflation it brought impoverished many who had lived off peasant rents fixed at uneconomic levels by the British government (see previous discussion). The British compounded their dilemma by requiring such landowners to "volunteer" their increasingly limited funds to the war effort. Finally, the war years provided many illegal or semi-legal opportunities (the black market, commodity hoarding, and rationing) for the smaller baniyas in Tezibazar to accumulate wealth. Thus at the very time that the landowning baniyas—no more than shadows of the traditional Hindu and Muslim overlords—were being depressed, the middling baniya merchants were being elevated.

When India became independent in 1947, no class existed in Tezibazar that could continue the traditional paternalism of the urban founders or even the reduced influence of the wealthy baniyas. The institution that came to perform somewhat similar functions, but in wholly new ways, penetrated the town from the outside. The conflicts between castes, families, and religious communities that had once been mediated by the overlords; the religious observances that they had formerly subsidized; and the urban status hierarchy that they had established and stabilized by their very existence—all these aspects of urban organization were now disputed or competed for within the ostensibly

democratic political apparatus of the prismatic state. The resolution of
family, lineage, and caste conflicts through municipal politics and electoral contests began in Tezibazar as early as 1922. However, the democratic government based on universal adult suffrage that India adopted
after independence accelerated this development and heightened the
conflict and competition that it produced. In the early 1960s, the following traditional conflicts defined the political sphere and public status
hierarchy in Tezibazar:

1. Two factions within a prestigious (patri-) lineage of a single
baniya caste—the Umar—opposed each other in municipal politics. The
antagonism between the Tribeni Lal faction and the Moti Lal faction was
at least several generations old; it arose from the "natural" enmity and
envy that exist when one segment of a lineage prospers while another
falls on harder times. Since this Umar lineage was and had always been
an influential and wealthy kin group in the town, its internal dissension became an ascriptive base that helped organize town-wide political
conflict. Before World War II, this antagonism was effectively suppressed by the influential baniya landlords, but since 1953 it has broken
into the public domain. In the municipal elections of that year as well as
all subsequent ones, members of the two factions have stood in political
opposition and have chosen candidates from within their own faction.

2. The above lineage—which we shall call the Chairman lineage—
has had a long history of conflict with another, the Leader lineage,
belonging to the same baniya caste. Over the last fifty years, the two
lineages have competed for precedence and control of the Umar caste,
both within Tezibazar and on a regional basis. Since 1948 they have also
opposed each other for office and influence in municipal politics. In this
contest, the Moti Lal faction from the Chairman lineage tends to side
with the Leader lineage against their own kinsmen of the Tribeni Lal
faction.

3. Caste conflict also entered the new political arena after independence in 1947. Wealthy leaders of various baniya castes competed in
politics by appealing to caste identity and mobilizing an electoral following around caste affiliation. The major caste conflict in municipal politics
pitted the aforementioned Umar against a loose confederation of smaller, less wealthy baniya castes such as the Jaiswal and Kesharvani, sometimes joined by the Tribeni Lal faction within the Chairman lineage.
The antagonism between these castes was also long-standing, and prob-
ably began with their competition for social precedence and commercial
control of the urban settlement created by Raja Udai Baks. Whatever its

origins, candidates in municipal elections depended on this animosity for votes. They thus defined an ascriptive constituency within the ostensibly nonascriptive political machinery of independent India.

Not all Tezibazar political leaders are compromised by family, lineage, or caste affiliation, however. In the early 1960s, a wealthy Brahman merchant who was an old-time Gandhian freedom fighter enjoyed considerable freedom in political maneuvering, as did a powerful Rajput who controlled the votes of many peasants in the countryside. Because they had a limited caste or kinship-determined electoral base in the town, these two political figures depended on their local organizational skills and their political contacts at the provincial and national levels for success. Their immediate aim was simply personal aggrandizement. This goal required them to become social brokers between the local caste and kinship antagonisms of municipal politics and the party politics of the wider society. Unlike the former overlords, such figures did not isolate the town from state politics; they did not act as buffers that resisted national pressures on their urban preserve. Rather, they were open channels for the penetration of national power, ideology, and politics into the local politics of traditional ascriptive conflicts.

The municipal election of 1953 will serve as an example of how national-level institutions intervened in local politics and, by extension, urban organization. In that year the wealthy Brahman merchant, Sita Ram, opposed the leader of the Chairman lineage, Tribeni Lal, for control of the municipal government. Tribeni Lal depended politically on wealth, personal prestige, and the support he could mobilize from his kin following and the loose collection of baniya castes mentioned above. Sita Ram also enjoyed wealth and personal prestige. However, without a sizable kin or caste following in Tezibazar, his major strength came from the connections he had long had with politicians and bureaucrats at the provincial and national levels. In the event, Tribeni Lal was elected to head the municipal government, and a period of severe political infighting began in Tezibazar. Until 1953, only one intermediate-level school (roughly equivalent to an American high school) had existed in the town. This school had been founded and thereafter managed by Tribeni Lal. In 1955, Sita Ram used his political connections at the provincial level to have government accreditation and financial subsidy of this school removed—an obvious and effective blow at his local political rival, Tribeni Lal. Sita Ram then organized another intermediate-level school in Tezibazar, and again used his political connections to have it quickly recognized and subsidized by the provincial government. The school confrontation greatly undermined Tribeni Lal's political following among the town population other than his own kinsmen. In 1956 he was unseated as head of the municipal government, and in the ensuing election, Sita Ram gained the post. Not only does this case show how personal ambition may be unhindered by preindustrial or industrial moral restraints, a condition typical of prismatic state societies; it also indicates how outside political forces may enter the unbridled competition of the local political arena and thereby condition colonial urban organization.

National politics creates new political confrontations in other ways, as is evident in the growing political antagonism between urban Muslims and Hindus. Although not an outgrowth of longstanding local caste and kin animosities, this conflict also has a heavy ascriptive content—one conditioned by communal religious identities. These identities have been increasingly manifested at the national level since the partition of India and Pakistan in 1947. Hindu-Muslim communal conflict in the form of organized political opposition did not really develop in Tezibazar until after the Second World War. The early years of the twentieth century witnessed sporadic violence and even riots between these two religious communities, usually over religious festivals and processions in the town. But these outbursts were short-lived and apolitical. After independence and the introduction of mass politics, these religious identities spawned violent but intermittent communal behavior. Both the religious identities and the communal behavior were increasingly channelled into urban political associations, which contested for political power. Because they were despised by the Hindu majority in the town, the Muslims were the first to organize politically. They developed a communal leadership that represented all Muslims, regardless of caste (at least fourteen Muslim castes exist in Tezibazar) or pedigree. This leadership suppressed individual conflict that threatened the unity of the community and controlled the bloc vote that the Muslims delivered in municipal and national elections. It espoused an ideology of secularism and tolerance against what Muslims saw as the religious persecution exercised by the Hindu majority. This ideological component is much more important in Muslim political association than in the caste and kinship politics of Tezibazar. In the latter, simple opposition to one's caste or kin opponent is all that matters, because the policies of national government are not at issue in the resolution of local antagonisms. Their greater ideological commitment strongly links the Muslims with the ruling Congress party because of its announced secular and egalitarian goals at the national level.

The Hindu castes in Tezibazar (most of whom are baniya) have undergone a similar development in opposition to the Muslims. They are driven together into communal political association by fear of the Muslim minority and by desire to counter the bloc vote that the Muslims can muster. However, because Hindus are in the majority and because preexisting kinship and caste conflicts sunder their unity, their association is much weaker. Nevertheless, this communal Hindu identity leads to strong links with a national party's ideology—in this case, the anti-Muslim, Hindu revivalism of the Jana Sangh party. Like Sita Ram's punitive use of provincial political connections to augment his local position, the development of local communal associations modeled after national religious antagonisms indicates how the prismatic qualities of the state society are directly refracted into the town.

The political developments in Tezibazar over the last century reflect the evolution of a preindustrial administrative town into a colonial urban locale. The traditional overlords, who administered the town and mediated its relations with the wider society, died out or became impoverished. They were eventually replaced by the ostensibly modern electoral machinery of independent India. The traditional caste and kin conflicts continue, however, and in fact are enhanced (because unresolved) in this new context. Other ascriptive associations, such as the Hindu and Muslim communities, develop in response to national political confrontation. They become more or less fixed to the ideology of particular political parties, hollow though this ideology may be. Thus, traditional loyalties to kin, caste, and religion continue to determine urban organization in Tezibazar. But they are employed in wholly new political contests for wealth and power within the prismatic state society.

Urban places in other prismatic states show the same evolution as Tezibazar. The Javanese town of Modjokuto studied by Clifford Geertz suffers from the stable "half-way" condition that also characterizes the peasantry once subject to the Culture System and the aborted plantation economy. Modjokuto's "advance toward vagueness," or what Geertz also calls its "spirited stagnation," parallels developments in Tezibazar:

> What replaced the [older] pattern was a series of cultural and social experiments, none of which could be solidly established and each of which, consequently, soon gave way to another in a bewildering whirl of directionless changes. The town . . . became stranded, in a state of continuous transition.
>
> . . . disorder at the very top of the society . . . was transmitted to the local level to render impossible both a full retreat to older patterns of living (though many still clung to what remained of these) or a genuine solidification of new ones (though many continued to try to construct them). And, as the disorder at the top accelerated . . . this spirited stag-

nation steadily increased until what had been movement became mere commotion.[19]

URBAN IDEOLOGY

Urban villagers and urban core populations espouse dissimilar
ideologies in colonial cities. The migrants enclaved within such cities
commonly find little permanent place for themselves in it. The baniyas
of Bombay, like other urban villagers, see their urban existence as
temporary and ephemeral (whether or not it is in reality). Their hearts
(and most of their incomes) are in the open plains and nucleated villages
of northern India where their kinsmen and families live. Similarly, in
Mexico City's vecindades, urban villagers display an apathy and cynicism
towards national government and little participation in urban associations. Whether or not the urban migrant will ever permanently return to
his village home, whether or not he even entertains this possibility, his
ideological ties to the city are weak. The urban place, he often feels,
leaves little mark on what he values or how he believes.

The urban villager puts *his* mark on the colonial city, however. The
overcrowded streets, shacks, and tenements of the migrant quarters,
with their lack of facilities, form a "slumscape" that is recent and yet
decayed. The squalid impoverishment of the urban villager as it shows in
urban spatial arrangements is testimony to the lack of industrial opportunity in the colonial city; it typifies the absence of industrial urbanization in the prismatic state.

The urban core population, sometimes rudely and at other times
willingly thrust into the politics of the prismatic state, does not scorn the
city. Social prestige, access to power and wealth, powerful political connections, and valuable commercial contacts are all to be gained in the
modern political arena—an arena that defines both the organization and
ideology of this core population. But faith in the new urban developments is not strong: At best, there is confusion and hesitation about
where these developments will lead; at worst, there is fear and distaste
for where they have already led. In Tezibazar, for example, urban
leaders speak of the present situation as one in which "money is every-
thing" and "might makes right." All public acts are considered to be
motivated by individual, kin, caste, or communal profit. The "new wind"
of greed and ambition has been criticized but necessarily endured by

[19]Geertz, *The Social History of an Indonesian Town*, pp. 4–5 and 151.

many citizens of Tezibazar. Others have embraced it. Thus this "new wind" prevails, and it leads to deep scepticism about the town's and the nation's future. This uncertainty, this sense of disequilibrium and disorientation, which Geertz also found in Modjokuto, clearly mirrors the condition of prismatic state society, caught perhaps permanently in the no-man's land between preindustrial and industrial patterns.

The colonial city represents an urban type that lacks an industrial economy and is therefore heavily dependent on the fossilized peasant agriculture of its surrounding rural areas. Such cities operate within the elaborate but hollow bureaucracy and the mass but communal politics of prismatic state societies. This disjuncture between political advancement and economic stagnation, both of which arise as legacies of former colonial status, means that such states refract preindustrial and industrial institutions into wholly new forms. The colonial city represents one of these forms. Urban villagers, having come as migrants from the stagnant countryside, remain unabsorbed and fall back on rural ways to succor them in the city. The disillusioned and disoriented urban core population, caught up in the hollow, ostensibly modern politics of the prismatic state, redefine ascriptive allegiances to kin, caste, or religion for competition in the new urban arena. Beset by overpopulation, political dissension, and economic insufficiency, these societies and their colonial cities, the last of our primary urban types, may not be the temporary phenomenon that many scholars and planners once imagined. Their expected slow movement toward modernization and industrialism now often appears to be simply directionless motion in place.

7

Industrial Cities

The greatest challenge now facing urban anthropology is the comprehension of cities that exist in the contemporary industrial and post-colonial world.[1] No anthropologist can be insensitive to the multitude of urban social problems that presently beset both the old industrial and the new industrializing nations and whose solutions may in part depend on scholarly analysis. But these cities also present a direct challenge to anthropology's future as an intellectual discipline and a scientific method of data collection: As the primitive world and peasant communities continue to disappear under the pressures of modernization and global industrialization, can anthropology in its scholarly conception and anthropologists as data-gatherers accommodate themselves to the emerging mainstream of human social life? Can they properly deal with the industrial and colonial city types?

Anthropologists in recent years have increasingly accepted this challenge—or at least part of it. They have gone to industrial cities, primarily in America, and collected quantities of social data on their inhabitants. These data clearly indicate that anthropological methods are appropriate to complex industrial urban environments. However,

[1]Some materials contained in this chapter originally appeared in Richard G. Fox, "Rationale and Romance in Urban Anthropology," *Urban Anthropology*, I, 2 (1972).

the part of the challenge that anthropologists have not yet met fully is the need for broad conceptual direction and theoretical goals in their study of industrial cities. What do we learn about industrial cities from the research on urban America? How can we compare the kind of urbanism that surrounds us with that of medieval Europe or pre-British India? The answers to these questions do not emerge from the anthropological research undertaken in industrial cities. Therefore these data cannot be used to construct an industrial urban type (or types) similar to the primary varieties of preindustrial and colonial urbanism discussed in previous chapters.

Nevertheless, a specific theoretical direction, which may eventually lead to formulation of an industrial urban type, is implicit in much anthropology done in industrial cities. This chapter notes this direction, its strength and liabilities, and suggests how this perspective might be augmented and vitalized by a holistic and comparative approach to the anthropology of industrial cities. Several concepts that link the urban anthropology commonly done in American cities with such a holistic viewpoint are offered in conclusion.

HETEROGENEITY AND THE INDUSTRIAL CITY

The typology of primary urbanism developed in Chapter Two indicates that the industrial function, or cultural role, of cities is associated with a highly bureaucratic state society. Such industrial states manifest a complexity in the organization of government and a power of intervention in the lives of their subjects unknown in preindustrial state societies. Such complexity and intervention would be impossible without the technological advances in communication, transportation, and weaponry that the Industrial Revolution brought. These industrial bureaucratic states enjoy a high degree of governmental specialization and a wide diversity of political institutions—with which we are all well acquainted by personal experience and by which we are often plagued. Presidents and police, judges and jailers, senators and civil servants, Pentagon and Cabinet, CIA and HEW, sheriffs and secretaries, all attest to the diversity and specialization of the industrial state and the wide distribution of its powers along a many-tiered and multi-linked bureaucracy.

If industrial cities are linked to their state societies by a process of adaptation similar to the urban accommodations found in preindustrial times, then we should expect a high degree of diversity and functional specialization to characterize industrial cities and to mark them as distinctive from other urban types. No great expertise is required to find this quality of diversity and specialization in American cities; scholars from many disciplines have noted and analyzed it for many years. In the urban context, the specialization and diversity of the industrial state society is termed "heterogeneity."

Heterogeneity—in terms of occupation, economic class, religious and political affiliation, leisure time activities, race and ethnicity, and social life in general—is a characteristic that has sometimes erroneously been imputed to all cities, but that most fully defines industrial urbanism.[2] The dense web of communication, transportation, and industrial production that coalesces in industrial cities and spreads out from them to encompass the wider society is an index of this heterogeneity within which most Americans act out their social lives. In this sense, heterogeneity implies specialization of function, a characteristic that achieves its highest levels within the urban context. The heterogeneity of occupational classes, the specialized institutions of education, politics, economy, and manufacture, the diversity of consumer goods and consumer tastes, clearly underlie the complex social life of an industrial state and its attendant cities.

The heterogeneity of industrial state societies has another aspect besides specialization. The very complexity of such societies and their cities means that heterogeneity often takes the form of separation, partial autonomy, and noncommunication or prejudice among its parts. For example, college-educated people tend to marry each other rather than randomly; suburban bridge clubs do not have members drawn from the ghetto poor. The major arterial highways surrounding our cities often whisk middle-class workers back to their bedroom communities without a glimpse of the inner-city population; ethnic associations are limited to those born of a specific parentage. All aspects of our cities and society evidence heterogeneity in the form of separation, autonomy, and prejudice; but some aspects imply greater disabilities for the populations involved than others. You may have to own a dog to join a kennel club or be a Democrat to attend the party's annual chicken barbecue— but the exclusiveness and social heterogeneity that underly these activities are not of the same punitive quality as that which ordains the poor to inferior education in neighborhood schools or the ethnic individual to substandard housing in an inner-city ghetto. An exclusion of certain classes, religions, races, and populations from full participation in the

[2]Cf. Wirth's and Redfield's definition of the city: Louis Wirth, "Urbanism as a Way of Life," *The American Journal of Sociology*, XLIV, 1 (1938), p. 8, and Robert Redfield, "The Folk Society," *The American Journal of Sociology*, LII, 4 (1947), p. 306.

society is associated with the heterogeneity of industrial states and their cities.

The implicit theoretical direction of most current anthropology in industrial cities is the study of this heterogeneity of excluded and under-privileged urban populations. It is the central motif in the "anthropology of urban poverty" approach noted in Chapter One. This theoretical direction remains implicit because the populations studied are often so fundamentally excluded from equal social participation that the urban anthropologist is enthralled with the non-mainstream social characteristics that these populations develop in response to their exclusion. As a result, the anthropologist's interest turns inward, and little of this research helps define or analyze the specific (industrial) urbanism in which this kind of heterogeneity exists.[3] Thus, ghetto and streetcorner studies in anthropology all indicate the great variability of life-ways, the variety of socialization patterns, and the extent of ethnic or racial heterogeneity and exclusiveness to be found in industrial urban life. This material is important because it documents the exclusiveness and exclusion of the poor, by-passed, and discriminated-against in our cities. But what do these disfranchised populations in ghettos, or these street corners filled with men who are cultured in poverty, tell us about industrial cities? That question remains unasked and unanswered in the anthropology of poverty. The heterogeneity that is discerned is used to characterize the population under study rather than to characterize the city that these populations inhabit. Once anthropologists of the ghetto find such heterogeneity to exist, they commonly pursue its content and expression (matrifocal families, juvenile gangs, black English, etc.) within the boundaries of the excluded populations rather than use it as an insight into the nature of industrial cities in their societies. Two detailed studies of disfranchised populations in American cities will illustrate the insights and limitations of this procedure.

Winston Street Ghetto

When Ulf Hannerz chose to do anthropological research among blacks on Winston Street, in Washington, D.C., his intention was to highlight those aspects of ghetto life that were most separate from

---

[3]Cf. Kenneth Moore, "The City as Context: Context as Process," *Urban Anthropology*, IV, 1 (Spring, 1975), p. 018: "Urban anthropology as it exists today is notable as a collection of ethnographies loosely related . . . unity of problem, to the degree that it exists, is best exemplified by the recurring void in the way the ethnographically studied part relates to the named but little understood urban whole."

mainstream America: "So [even] if the outside society has . . . integrated the ghetto with itself politically and economically, then family life,
leisure life, and just plain neighborship remain largely separated. These
are the spheres in which a community social structure peopled only by
ghetto dwellers is built up."[4]

This emphasis on ghetto distinctiveness requires Hannerz "to neg-
lect"[5] social relationships in the ghetto that follow mainstream patterns.
There are good reasons why an anthropologist interested in industrial
cities might wish to make this purposeful selection of the heterogeneity
and separateness of the ghetto. He might want, for example, to measure
how much heterogeneity exists or is possible in American (industrial)
cities, at least insofar as the ghetto represents the furthest limits of
distinctiveness. But Hannerz, like many others who follow the anthropology of poverty approach, does not provide this kind of justification for his study. He falls back on a romantic justification of anthropology's quest for all varieties of human society: "It has always been
one of the duties of anthropology to show that whether a way of life is
like your own or not, it is a reasonable and understandable combination
of common human themes."[6]

This justification limits urban anthropology to mere description,
not explanation or even comprehension. It represents a common attitude (whether conscious or not) among the anthropologists of the ghetto
who strive to maintain their small-scale and synchronic anthropological
traditions. But in return for the security of studying ghettos and other
heterogenetic groups in industrial society as if they were primitive tribes,
this urban anthropology cannot say why ghettos exist, only that they do;
cannot explain how the heterogeneity mirrored in the ghetto develops
or is maintained, only that it does and is. Although anthropologists are
increasingly recognizing the limitations of this approach, it is important
to understand the present state of the anthropology of industrial cities.
We have several excellent studies of the ghetto and of disfranchised
populations that focus on the internal aspects of their variant life-ways;
we have few that relate their descriptions to the characteristics of industrial or American cities. Assuming that such studies in the anthropology
of the ghetto represent the goals and directions of all urban anthropology is as likely *and* egregious a mistake as assuming all anthropology to be
the study of primitive societies after reading Malinowski on the Tro-
briands or Lowie on the Crow.

Because he is a sensitive observer, Hannerz, like others who follow

[4]Ulf Hannerz, *Soulside: Inquiries into Ghetto Culture and Community* (New York:
Columbia University Press, 1969), p. 12.
[5]*Ibid.*, pp. 15–16.
[6]*Ibid.*, p. 16.

this form of urban anthropology, provides many excellent insights into ghetto life. This work is important as a source of raw data, even if one disagrees with the anthropologist who collects the material as to how it can be used. Thus Hannerz documents the great separation of some ghetto life-styles and social behavior from mainstream American patterns; he gives us an empirical base from which to judge the heterogeneity incorporated into American (industrial) cities.

Hannerz distinguishes four typical ghetto life-styles: those lived by mainstreamers, swingers, street families, and streetcorner men. Mainstreamers are generally stably employed, married homeowners. Their life-style conforms to mainstream American urban expectations more closely than others in the ghetto. In their consumption of furniture, appliances, and other consumer goods; in the interior decoration of their houses with family pictures and china figurines; in their regular reading of newspapers and magazines for the home, mainstreamers evidence a concern for social status, family propriety, and the "good things in life" that most Americans identify as their goals.

Swingers are young, unmarried or unattached persons who like to party (Hannerz reports that one swinger attended nine parties in one night). Their way of life is highly mobile, both in personal relations, in which they form and break marital or consensual unions frequently, and in residence and employment, in which they shift from job to job or from one apartment to another. Their wide personal networks bring them into contact with many people and activities throughout the ghetto.

The life-style of street families represents a major departure from the American urban mainstream. Street families are child-rearing units with high incidences of consensual unions or female-headed households containing several generations of related adult women. Ghetto people with this life-style are often poverty-stricken, unemployed and on welfare, or in unskilled jobs. Household composition is variable and ever-changing. Marriages and consensual unions break; economic necessity brings in paying boarders or unattached kinsmen, such as brothers. Ties between household members are correspondingly loose, especially in the relationship between spouses. Husbands interact within a peer group of other men; wives, more attached to the household by child-rearing and domestic duties, interact with a circle of close kinsmen.

The life-style of the streetcorner men is another example of the separation of the ghetto from mainstream ways. Men who evidence this life-style are often recent migrants from the South, generally poorly educated unskilled laborers who are often unemployed. Their lives are measured out in peer group interaction with male cronies on the streetcorners and in pool halls, carry-outs, and selected meeting houses of the ghetto. Usually unattached, streetcorner men are often boarders with no permanent residence. Alcohol, cards, and comradeship are the common elements developed by these men in peer group relations; robbery, violence, and police records are the common attributes of their life-style.[7]

This range of life-styles indicates how social behavior deemed reprehensible in the wider society may be accepted in the ghetto, often as an economic adaptation to the poverty and the unstable employment characteristics of its inhabitants. Hannerz documents other instances in which the ghetto's way of life is separate from or even directly contradictory to mainstream urban patterns. In the case of male self-definition, common American values of toughness, sexuality, and drinking ability are heightened into the more elaborated ghetto version of hard drinking, violence, fast talking, fancy dressing, and widespread but impermanent sexual interactions. A highly developed form of verbal dueling—which Hannerz calls "rituals of obscenity"—also channels ghetto adolescent interactions in ways unlike those of the wider society. The exchange of insults termed "sounding" or "joining" occurs between two or more boys who toss stereotyped pejorative (and usually obscene) remarks about each other's families back and forth. Hannerz also notes the importance of socialization outside the domestic unit. Street life, the hostility to white society, the general suspicion of people's motives, and the importance of concepts such as soul and the music that expresses it are important ways in which ghetto life is separate and autonomous from mainstream America.

Hannerz thus powerfully documents the exclusiveness of the Winston Streeters within the American city. But his major concern is to describe their variant life-styles rather than to take this description as illustrating or exemplifying anything in the city. We do not learn to what degree this exclusiveness is possible or practiced by other urban residents (do mainstream urbanites really live all that differently from ghetto people?). We cannot tell whether the conditions of Winston Street apply to all poor people, or all blacks in Washington, D.C., or whether the same life-styles exist in the ghettos of Detroit or Los Angeles. In short, the material on Winston Street, illuminating and descriptive as it is, has no holistic context into which it can be placed.

Skid Road Alcoholics

James Spradley's study of urban alcoholics along Skid Road in Seattle has many of the same strengths and weaknesses that are found in the Winston Street material. Spradley specifies the heterogeneity of

[7]*Ibid.*, pp. 54–57.

exclusion even further by proposing that a culture or subculture of urban alcoholism exists. This subculture makes urban nomads (as he terms these people) different from mainstream Americans: "The distance between most Americans and urban nomads cannot be measured in miles; they are separated from us by *cultural distance*. Their style of life is not only strange but also abhorrent to most Americans."[8] Spradley uses this cultural argument to plead for an American cultural relativism that respects and values such urban nomadism as a different way of life. His objective thus becomes a description of this distinctive culture. Like Hannerz's, Spradley's rationale for this urban anthropology contains no goals related to the analysis of cities or how their component groups interact to define the urban sphere: "As anthropologists turn their attention to urban subcultures they are bringing with them a guiding principle, gained by studying hundreds of so-called 'primitive' societies: *discover the native point of view*."[9]

The separate and alienated culture that Spradley describes in discussing urban nomads bears a strong resemblance to the culture of poverty analyzed by Oscar Lewis. Their argument is that these cultures are so distinctive and so deviant from mainstream patterns that individuals within them are socialized to have values, orientations, and behaviors that prevent attainment of American cultural expectations. Thus Spradley finds that urban nomads define a cultural world and have for that world an elaborate expressive terminology that depends on their mobile, impoverished, and alienated life-style. For example, elaborate verbal categories used by urban nomads classify tramps into working stiffs, mission stiffs, boxcar tramps, dings, and so forth on the basis of their mobility, mode of travel, home base, livelihood, and other criteria. An equally discriminating classification exists among urban nomads for different jail duties performed when "in the tank" as well as for different sorts of "flops," or sleeping places (paid flops, weed patch flops, railroad flops, mission flops, etc., and subcategories of each).[10]

Spradley suggests that individuals are socialized into this culture of urban nomadism by the prejudice and discrimination of the larger society, specifically by the police, the courts, and the jails. He shows, for instance, that judges reinforce the mobility of urban nomads by giving lighter sentences to those who promise to leave town. He indicates how the jail experience selects for passivity and other behaviors that con the system but leave the urban nomad that much more alienated and impoverished.

[8]James P. Spradley, *You Owe Yourself a Drunk: An Ethnography of Urban Nomads* (Boston: Little, Brown and Company, 1970), p. 6.
[9]*Ibid.*, p. 7.
[10]*Ibid.*, pp. 100–104.

There can be little question that the urban dwellers subsumed under Lewis's culture of poverty and Spradley's urban nomadic culture are oppressed and alienated populations whose behavior does not follow mainstream expectations. Much more argument concerns whether these populations constitute separate cultures or subcultures.[11] Lewis and Spradley argue that the values and behaviors evidenced are so different and deviant that individuals must be socialized into them in a more or less irrevocable manner, just as Hindus are brought up to live in Indian society and the children of the Manus are taught their own life-ways. However, another equally plausible explanation is that there is nothing irrevocable or cultural in the values and behaviors of urban nomads; that their life-style is a situational adaptation to the exigencies of poverty, disfranchisement, and the disease of alcoholism. If they could be removed from the constant social and psychological pressures under which these behaviors are adaptive, they would be similar to any other urban dweller of the American mainstream.

Elliot Liebow makes the best statement of this alternative to the culture concept when he interprets ghetto behavior as a skewed variant of mainstream American values, the closest that people can obtain given the poverty, unstable and demeaning employment, lack of education, and prejudice under which they suffer:

> . . . the stretched or alternative value systems [of the ghetto] are not the same order of values, either phenomenologically or operationally, as the parent or general system of values [in the larger society]: they are derivative, subsidiary in nature . . . less completely internalized and seem to be value images reflected by forced or adaptive behavior rather than real values with a positive determining influence on behavior . . . a shadow cast by the common value system in the distorting lower-class setting.[12]

The situational interpretation would thus see the specialized and elaborate terminologies of Spradley's urban nomad as simple adaptations to the conditions under which they live. Such terminologies would be judged to be no different from the specialized jargons and knowledge of the heterogeneous occupational groups of our society such as farmers (how many different sorts of cows or soils can one distinguish?) or printers (what are the varieties of type faces called?), except that preju-

---

[11]See Charles A. Valentine, *Culture and Poverty: Critique and Counter-Proposals* (Chicago: University of Chicago Press, 1968), pp. 107–120, and Hannerz, *Soulside*, pp. 193–95.
[12]Elliot Liebow, *Tally's Corner: A Study of Negro Streetcorner Men* (Boston: Little, Brown and Company, 1967), p. 213n.

dice and disease (alcoholism) are major factors in their lives and therefore in their language.

These two conflicting interpretations have waxed and waned among anthropologists for the last ten years, the current favorite dependent in part on the political persuasion of the scholar and in part on the political climate of the times. This issue cannot be resolved with any certainty given the anthropological research on industrial or American cities carried out up to now within the anthropology of poverty approach. Resolving this question requires a holistic viewpoint of the organization of heterogeneity in American industrial cities. We need some measure or index of the kinds of heterogeneity that are typical or possible within a constructed industrial urban type. Such an index could be compared with empirical cases. A judgment could then be made about whether the deviance exemplified in the ghetto or urban nomad is so great as to require an irrevocable socialization and thereby becomes cultural, or whether the deviance is simply an extreme variant of the situational specialization and heterogeneity typical of the industrial city. In other words, the holistic approach would tell us where such populations and their life-styles fit within the context of industrial urban organization.

Unfortunately, the anthropology of poverty, as exemplified in the work of Hannerz and Spradley, does not aim for these goals. Its priority is simply to provide a descriptive base of ghetto life and urban nomad ways. In the case of Spradley and Lewis, this approach must fall back on the culture concept to provide some rationale for its limited interests. Such research, excellent and sensitive as it often is, must still be complemented by a holism along the lines suggested in our chapters on preindustrial urbanism. The next section of this chapter gives an example of this holism by contrasting two American cities and their pattern of external adaptation to the industrial America growing up around them. The final section then suggests how the microlevel approach of the anthropology of poverty can be merged with the holistic approach of the anthropology of urbanism to the improvement of both.

URBAN VARIATION
IN INDUSTRIAL AMERICA

The contemporary organizations and ideologies of American cities derive in part from their differing colonial pasts. This historical dimension is one important determinant of (secondary) urban variability within industrial America. The following pages briefly contrast the political histories of two American cities—Newport, Rhode Island, and Charleston, South Carolina—and the way their external adaptations have conditioned present-day urban organization and ideology.

Two basic types of local government evolved in the English colonies of North America from the early 1600s on, and greatly influenced the subsequent pattern of urban development. The first type is found in the New England region, where the town meeting developed as the method of local administration. Although scholars disagree about how democratically this system operated, town meetings gave a great amount of independence and initiative to local civic authorities at the same time that they restricted the authority of town officers. A contrasting type of local administration developed in the remaining American colonies. Here the country or parish system of government obtained, and urban areas when they developed were administered within the county or parish political framework. Especially in the colonial South but also elsewhere outside New England, therefore, urban locales constituted administered urban places that developed as adjuncts of central government. They never achieved an independent municipal identity along the lines of the New England town meeting.[13] Newport, Rhode Island, represents an urban political adaptation in industrial America emerging from the New England pattern. Charleston, South Carolina, reflects urban development out of a monolithic colonial government.

Nonpartisans and the City
Over the Bridge

Newport has not always been a city on the other side of a bridge from the major part of Rhode Island. In an earlier period, transportation links between the seaport city at the southern tip of Aquidneck Island and the rest of the state were solely by water. But the bridge provides a physical symbol of Newport's separation from the northern part of the state. For many Newporters, "anything that comes over the bridge is bad," a statement that signifies their distaste for the intrusion of the governmental power and economic supremacy that is lodged in the Providence area. Their distate has endured from the time the state capital was moved from Newport and the Rhode Island economy shifted from seaport mercantilism to inland industrialism. The statement also reflects an urban ideology that accentuates Newport's former glory and present "cosmopolitanism," as distinct from the working-class provin-

---

[13]Conrad M. Arensberg and Solon T. Kimball, *Culture and Community* (NewYork: Harcourt, Brace & World, Inc., 1965).

cialism of the northern country over the bridge. This desire for autonomy, this symbolic and, at times in the past, physical resistance to the
"other" Rhode Island has its organizational analogue in the contemporary nonpartisan city manager municipal government. This municipal
government formally, and in the expectation of many residents, actually,
removes Newport from (state) party politics.

Throughout the history of the town and, subsequently, city of
Newport, a nonpartisan style of local government has been the ideal of
many citizens.Their advocacy is not only or even mainly based on the
merits of this form of municipal organization for the internal direction
of the city. Nonpartisanship for many Newporters has to do with re-
moving them from the flow of politics in the rest of Rhode Island. Town
or city government is expected to concern itself with internal arrangements only; both formal governmental links between state and city and
informal party links are best avoided. In a recognizably American combination of political naïveté and belief in the moral worth of commerce,
the cry in Newport has always been that party politics has no place in a
city. A city's proper government, instead, must rest on businesslike
principles.

An ideological and interactional tradition of autonomy lies behind
this pursuit of the nonpartisanship. Although the constitution of Rhode
Island makes Newport an urban creation of the state, the city at present
and in the past often acted as if its existence and organization were solely
at local discretion. The city's political history, including the first (abor-
tive) charter shortly after the American Revolution as well as its successful incorporation in 1853, involves a never-ending contest between state
authority and local autonomy, the last installment of which occurred as
recently as 1970. This contest, indicative of Newport's lack of synchroni-
zation with the state, is partially explained by its economic dependence
on external sources such as the nonlocal wealthy elite, the so-called
"summer colonists," and more recently, the United States Navy. This
economic reliance on the outside explains much of Newport's "cosmopolitan" outlook; it also explains why Newport's interests have often
diverged from the rest of Rhode Island.

A political heritage also helps explain the nonpartisan tradition.
The Newport town meeting antedates the formation of the colony of
Rhode Island by several decades. It was only with reluctance and the
reservation of many local powers that the town of Newport agreed to
join Providence and other newly settled areas to form a colonial government under the royal charter of 1663. Since that time, the town form
of local government has continued to play an important role in Rhode
Island. Although a division into formal counties exists, these counties
have relatively few functions and bear no resemblance to the importance

of the county elsewhere, especially in the South. Newport carefully guarded its prerogatives as a town, and having become a city continued to believe in its autonomy. Both in 1784 and from 1847 to 1853, attempts at incorporation seem generated by a desire to remove Newport from state politics and policies, which in both periods were moving in a direction hostile to Newport's interests. Incorporation was resisted by a combination of those who did not want such isolation from the state and others, stauncher nonpartisans, who feared any attempt to abridge the powers of the town meeting. Over the past 125 years the sentiment for autonomy has often lost out to a more organic structure of state and city government or politics. Nevertheless, the nonpartisans of Newport have continually reasserted themselves. In 1953, they won their greatest success by passage of a home rule charter that established a nonpartisan city manager form of local administration. However, this system is not completely secured; it has been continually challenged up to the present by those who wish to see Newport politics defined in the image of the state. Many residents feel that the next swing in a cyclical alternation between party politics and nonpartisanship (which they perceive only in its most recent form) will shortly be upon them.

The pursuit of nonpartisanship in Newport establishes the adaptive pattern of the city: a retreat from outside political domination through creation of political forms divergent from the rest of Rhode Island, a reservation of the city for its residents and their economic pursuits whether or not the "other" Rhode Island concurs—in short, a bounding of the city as an enclave within the state. No dreams of empire have ever come from Newport, as they did from Charleston. The symbol of the bridge, like the Chinese Wall, marks off what is without from what is within. It indicates a political and economic insularity that the nonpartisans of Newport have taken pains to establish or maintain throughout the city's development.

The relationship of Newport to its governmental hinterland is reflected in the urban organization of the city. The shift in political power and economic preeminence to the Providence area not only threatened the civic autonomy Newport enjoyed as a heritage of the town meeting system, but also indirectly promoted changes in its urban class structure. Over the last century this class structure has reinforced the decentralized and nonpartisan spirit of city government, a spirit ultimately derived from the town meeting system. The dislocations of the Revolution, the end of the slave trade, and the rise of the port of New York all eliminated Newport's prosperity and removed most of her resident elite. Absence of a local elite for whom the city might serve as a power base in politics at the state level, coupled with the desire of the summer colonists for "cheap and honest" government, acted against the machine politics of the ethnic minorities. Newport therefore maintained a decentralized and "representative" municipal government. In the early twentieth century for example, city government consisted of over two hundred elected representatives drawn from a total population of under twenty-five thousand. Just as the present class composition of the city shows no elite domination of politics, so the contemporary city manager system (which puts urban administration into the hands of an apolitical specialist) continues a former weak-mayor organization. It also reflects the even earlier decentralization of the town meeting.

The municipal history of Newport is thus a never-ending cycle of charter alterations and changes in the structure of city government—sometimes promoted by increasing intervention from Providence, at other times generated by local antipathy to external domination. The analogue of the eternal quest for autonomy is the pursuit of decentralized civic authority within the city. In the absence of controlling power groups within the urban area, electoral alliances with state parties or factions are minimized. Thus, the wish for local autonomy and the desire for internal decentralization intertwine and reinforce each other. Their interdependency defines the adaptive pattern of Newport as a city of nonpartisans with a characteristic view of their political hinterland as "over the bridge."

Nabobs and the Holy City

Charleston achieved municipal incorporation after the American Revolution, although an earlier charter of 1722 was in force for a year before the colonial legislature countermanded it. During almost the entire colonial period, the urban area was directly administered by the colonial legislature working through parish organization and special urban commissions. When the incorporated city did emerge in Charleston, it was a small-scale replica of the state, centralizing the same powers of social control, being staffed by the same class that controlled state government, and having the same responsibility for controlling an internal population that the state had for controlling an external one.

The early history of South Carolina government (up to 1808) consisted of attempts by the minority low-country slave-owning planters to dominate politically the majority up-country small-scale farmers. The farmers in turn disliked the slavery, aristocratic airs, and grandiose economic consumption of the Coast. The colonial and early state government of South Carolina was in large measure only an agency of control over these potential dissidents in the "uncultured" hinterland to the west. Because the urban area of Charleston was the physical location of the colonial capital, and because the leaders of the state legislature were also the wealthy "nabobs" who formed the elite of the city, colonial government in South Carolina was the medium by which the Charleston "city-state" controlled its western territories.

Incorporation of the city of Charleston was in the same way an attempt to control another group of dissidents, in this case the radical artisans of Charleston. These radical artisans had grown vocal during the American Revolution and had become increasingly militant (and riotous) as resumption of imports from England and the use of slaves in artisan trades threatened their existence.[14] Rather than the result of a desire for municipal autonomy as was the case in Newport, Charleston city was chartered as a special arm of state government, charged at its outset with the maintenance of public safety (which meant, in effect, the suppression of the radical artisans). Even though city and state were organizationally separate, they were, in fact, a single political structure in the sense of a continuity of centralized and elitist administration, and in the sense of an interlocking directorate of low-country nabobs who controlled both city and state. These nabobs formed a self-conscious group linked to each other as much by clubs, dance balls, and other pageants as by economic purpose and political power. Some Charlestonians compare themselves at present to the Chinese because "we eat rice and worship our ancestors." Not only a statement of cuisine and religion, this saying lays bare the economic base and elite organization that made Charleston city and South Carolina state long inseparable in a way Newport and Rhode Island never were.

The structure of city government replicates the organization of the state, and until very recently, few other governmental bodies intermediated between city and state government. Charleston's municipal organization has long been highly centralized, with a de facto strong-mayor system even when this form was not permitted by state statute. City government has been remarkably stable in formal constitution. It has been characterized by severe fighting between elite factions or personal cliques rather than clashes between contesting political ideologies. The relationship of Charleston to state government has been sometimes friendly and sometimes hostile, but the city has always recognized the outside as an important constraint on its power and as a further avenue for political ambition. Before the War Between the States, its links to the external world were predatory and paternalistic: South Carolina state was an extension of the city, and Charleston provided both political resistance and cultural style to the pre-Civil War South. Even in the last

---

[14]Richard Walsh, *Charleston's Sons of Liberty: A Study of the Artisans, 1763–1789* (Columbia: University of South Carolina Press, 1959).

hundred years—when in the aftermath of the Civil War and the popu-
lism of the late nineteenth and twentieth centuries, Charleston has ceased
to dominate South Carolina, when its power and paternalism have
waned—the city has not walled itself off from state politics. Rather, its
formal organization seeks to limit outside control by a replication of state
political forms. Through a strong machine politics, which was often both
corrupt and violent, Charleston has been able to guarantee votes to
various state-wide candidates, and thus has won favors at the same time
that it protected local autonomy. Only in the last two decades has a
burgeoning county government intervened and altered Charleston's
ability to cope with the outside.

The continuity of state and city in the past and the duplication of
state powers in city government have promoted in Charleston a predatory and/or repressive adaptive pattern in respect to the larger society and
to segments of the urban population. Charleston's urban organization
represses the black population of the inner city, just as in former days it
repressed the slave populace who worked the low country plantations
and served in the nabobs' town houses. Blacks' separation and removal
from the body politic were symbolized in the past by legal disfranchisement. Today an urban organization of politics and city redistricting
renders their almost-majority electoral weight ineffective and keeps
them isolated from the political currents of state and city.

Throughout its history, fear of the black majority has conditioned
Charleston's urban organization, internal class divisions, and relations
with a changing external world. Electoral suppression of the up-country
white majority and physical suppression of the slaves mandated the
centralization of South Carolina as well as the city. But there must be
accommodation with one or another of these populations. The nabobs
of early Charleston had to choose whether blacks would be used to
contain up-country whites or vice versa. After the exportation of the
slave system westward in the early eighteenth century, Charleston compromised and allied with the up-country whites. This alliance weakened
the city relative to the state (by geographically and organizationally
separating the latter from city domination) and generated the problems
that now beset the urban area.

At present, Charleston is encircled by up-country whites attracted
to local industry. These whites have rejected the city and its pattern and
incorporated as an independent city. Today's Charleston has reacted to
this most recent threat from the outside in a fashion characteristic of its
past: by predation and political maneuvering. The city has urged creation of a consolidated government over the whole of Charleston County.
Many people see this proposal as only a device for the extension of the
city's power over an area that it desperately needs to counteract inner-

city black poverty and increasing black voting power—an area that is unlike Charleston in population origins and life-style. The last Congressional elections witnessed an alliance of the sort that Charleston has always most feared: one between city blacks and hinterland whites to circumvent the choice of the city's political leadership. Whether the final outcome will be an expanded and consolidated Charleston or a prosperous separate city in the northern suburbs that will economically strangle the old town has not yet been resolved. The methods of battle and the contesting ideologies of city and suburb reflect three hundred years of Charleston's urban organization and external adaptation.

Fear of the black majority within and the white majority without has played an important role in the class organization of Charleston. At several points in its history, the city has been confronted with internal populist and radical activism by whites. The city elite has always feared an alliance of these people with either city blacks or up-country whites. Consequently it has moved quickly to suppress these groups or to make its own alliance up-country to undermine their potential power sources. Time and again, Charleston has reverted to a political two-class condition in which no intermediary groups exist between urban elite and urban slave/black. The radical artisans of the post-Revolutionary period were put down by electoral suppression, economic competition from blacks, and absorption through intermarriage with the elite.

After the Civil War, a new generation of radical artisans appeared, in this case Irish Catholic immigrants who came to "Little Mexico" (so named for its bloody battles rather than ethnic composition) and other urban ethnic enclaves. At first, Charleston met the threat of carpetbaggers and Reconstruction government by attempts at alliance with blacks. However, later, in response to Hampton's Red Shirt movement at the state level, the urban elite played ethnic politics with the immigrant white population to disfranchise the former slaves. The political power of these immigrants grew, especially after their alliance with up-country whites; but after the First World War they were suppressed through the use of the Ku Klux Klan. Charleston again became a two-class city. This condition has continued into the present because of gradual enrichment and social acceptance of former immigrants, the exodus of middle-class whites to the suburbs after World War II, and the higher reproduction rate and lack of residential mobility of the black population. In the 1960s Charleston met this problem by incorporating some of the white suburbs, although with much opposition and only limited success. In 1971, an alliance of inner-city blacks with white leadership in the suburbs threatened to unseat the ruling clique that had controlled the city since 1959. In conjunction with this internal threat came the external problem of its unincorporated white hinterland promoting a county government that infringed the city's political ties with the state, and then achieving a separate incorporation, which undermines the city's economic base. These contemporary dilemmas repeat situations that the city has often seen before in its long-standing attempts at balancing and controlling internal class dissension and external adaptation. It remains to be seen whether Charleston's equally long urban adaptive pattern of absorption, predation, and suppression will be equal to these current tasks.

The Newport and Charleston materials reflect a holistic view of secondary urban variability in industrial America. They help tell us why specific cities have different organizations and ideologies even though they are set within a common industrial state society. The portrayal of Charleston and Newport also illustrates a level of analysis very different from the anthropology of the ghetto exemplified by Winston Street and Skid Road. The ghetto studies illustrate the heterogeneity of life-styles that exists in industrial cities at the microlevel, whereas the anthropology of the two American cities neglects this internal heterogeneity. It emphasizes variant urban adaptive patterns within industrial America in the widest perspective. Skid Road and ghetto street are submerged in the latter urban anthropology, just as the differences between Washington and Seattle within American industrial urbanism are lost in the former. Neither approach avoids liabilities; both offer valuable insights. The dilemma is how to combine the two viewpoints into an effective anthropology of industrial cities. The following section attempts to answer this question.

OVERVIEW AND UNDERVIEW
IN URBAN ANTHROPOLOGY

What are the links between an urban anthropology that looks at entire cities and one that focuses on the separate and excluded populations within such cities? That is the crux of the problem in accommodating the "overview" of a holistic anthropology of (industrial) urbanism with the "underview" of the anthropology of urban poverty.

The analysis of Charleston and Newport suggests the direction this accommodation might take. The organization of social classes and the exclusion (or inclusion) of specific ethnic or racial populations within urban politics are portrayed, in our analysis, as reflections of the external adaptions of these cities. In Charleston, the old WASP and Huguenot elite aligned with the new Irish Catholic and German immigrants after the Civil War to defeat the urban black electoral majority. Fifty

er, this elite called on state government and the Ku Klux Klan to
ss the ethnic (mainly Catholic) machine that had come to dominate urban politics. Irish Catholic immigrants in Newport organized
powerful ward political machines at roughly the same period in the
nineteenth century. But the Newport ethnics took over urban politics by
cementing party and patronage ties at the state level. These ties contra-
vened the Newport elite and its policy of separation. Thus, the organization and treatment of specific urban populations—ghetto dweller,
ethnic, alcoholic, black—are in some respects reflections of the specific
external adaptation of the given city. By concentrating on the relationship of excluded, impoverished, and disfranchised populations (or
wealthy, included, and powerful groups) to the adaptive patterns of the
cities they inhabit, anthropologists can mold overview and underview in
urban anthropology into a powerful analysis of industrial cities.

The anthropologist in the field can study the relationship between
ghetto and city in two ways: (1) through the "adaptive strategies" utilized
by ethnic, racial, or other populations to achieve power, security, or
status within specific cities; and/or (2) through the individuals or institutions that act as brokers or middlemen between ghetto or excluded
populations and formal urban institutions such as the police, labor
unions, and various industries. Ulf Hannerz developed the concept of
adaptive strategies to analyze how different ethnic populations compete
in American cities.[15] He suggests three such strategies:

1. Ethnic dominance: where ethnic groups monopolize certain activities or occupations as avenues for social mobility.

2. Ethnic entrepreneurship: where individuals exploit their
   ethnic identity to gain clienteles or make commercial connections.

3. Ethnic brokerage: where individuals use common ethnicity
   to mobilize political followings, work groups, or voluntary
   associations.

Because of his primary interest in the ghetto "underview," Hannerz does not deal with the specific urban conditions under which one or
another of these strategies may be promoted. But as the Charleston and
Newport material clearly indicates, the particular historical and demographic pattern of given American cities will determine in large measure
the adaptive strategy pursued by any ethnic population. By studying
such adaptive strategies, the anthropologist can see not only the accom-

[15]Ulf Hannerz, "Ethnicity and Opportunity in Urban America," in *Urban Ethnicity*,
Abner Cohen, ed. (London: Tavistock Publications, 1974).

modation of ethnic population to the city, but also the external tion and organization of the city as they affect this accommodation.

The study of middlemen and brokers focuses on a compleme ..ary linkage between ghetto and city. Brokers and middlemen are individuals or institutions operating partly in the ghetto and partly within the wider urban locale as conduits of information, power, money, and prestige from one sphere to the other. Although clearly recognized by anthropologists working within the "underview" perspective, such agents or agencies are often neglected by these anthropologists because the mediating character of the agents means they do not follow "typical" ghetto patterns. Thus, Winston Street is linked through bootleggers, numbers runners, ethnic political leaders, and ministers to the wider Washington scene, but their role as mediators and its effects on ghetto organization and ideology are only noted by Hannerz in passing reference. Similarly, they may be neglected in a holistic anthropology of the city because they are different from the urban mainstream. Yet their characteristics in any American city must necessarily reflect its adaptive pattern and its setting within an industrial society. Robert Dahl has pointed out this fact most clearly in his study of New Haven, Connecticut. He describes it as a city of "dispersed inequalities," where the former political oligarchy of the elite has been replaced by a fragmentation of political access.[16] Just as the middlemen and brokers are bridges between ghetto and city, so too an urban anthropology that analyzes their activities would link the anthropology of (industrial) urbanism with the anthropology of poverty.[17]

This chapter has perforce been more discursive and polemical than previous ones. In this respect it is a faithful reflection of the dissimilar and sometimes contradictory theoretical currents that presently flow through the urban anthropologies undertaken in American industrial cities and through the field of urban anthropology in general. However diverse these viewpoints, they show anthropologists pursuing answers to the major questions in urban research: What can anthropology contribute to our understanding of cities? What do studies of urban populations

[16]Robert A. Dahl, *Who Governs?: Democracy and Power in an American City* (New Haven: Yale University Press, 1964), p. 86.

[17]For similar formulations of the integration of overview and underview in American urban anthropology, see Jack R. Rollwagon, "The City as Context: The Puerto Ricans of Rochester, New York," *Urban Anthropology*, IV, 1 (Spring, 1975), pp. 053–060; and M. Estellie Smith, "A Tale of Two Cities: The Reality of Historical Differences," *Urban Anthropology* IV, 1 (Spring, 1975), pp. 061–072.

contribute to anthropology? These separate but related questions—most immediately compelling in the study of industrial cities but relevant to all urban locales—are at the heart of any future urban anthropology.

At the present moment the second question is more readily answered than the first. City studies offer anthropologists a future, perhaps the only and surely the most important future for a discipline bereft of the primitive world that comprised its earliest and formative subject matter. As the world continues to urbanize—whether as urban villagers or into industrial megalopolises—anthropology must also urbanize its scholarly activities if it is to remain the study of on-going human societies. To recognize the absolute necessity of urban studies for anthropology's future ought not discount all that anthropology has already accomplished in the study of primitive societies and peasant communities. A scholarly discipline without a past is just as deficient as one lacking a future.

For this precise reason, the first question—what can anthropology as distinct from other social sciences say about cities?—requires an answer based on the insights anthropology has developed into human societies, insights now taken from the most primitive and applied to the most complex. This difficult question has led urban anthropologists to several different theoretical and methodological positions on urban research, as we have seen. Yet since each of these urban anthropologies studies a separate aspect of urban life—urbanism, poverty, or urbanization—with distinctly anthropological methods and viewpoint, they all equally answer the question of what anthropology can add to urban studies. But a truly effective urban anthropology cannot be content with this condition of "separate but equal." Urbanism, poverty, and urbanization are all aspects of a single phenomenon, the city. Thus they can be combined into a general anthropological view of what cities are and how urban social institutions develop and function under different social conditions. This task, which is the ultimate answer to how anthropology can enhance scholarship on cities and how city studies can guarantee anthropology's future, remains to be done. Because such a task has yet to be accomplished, this introduction to urban anthropology has necessarily been more than simply a summary of past accomplishments (which are necessarily few) and present orientations (which are multiple). It has organized materials still in the process of formation and suggested where urban anthropology might go (rather than where it has been) and why this direction should be followed. This task is not easy and therefore our answers may be found wanting; however, this volume does suggest an orientation that integrates the various viewpoints current in urban anthropology.

The general framework for this book has come from the anthropology of urbanism approach: a holistic view of cities and the societies in which they are set and within which they perform distinctive cultural roles; a cross-cultural view that compares these urban cultural roles in different times and places. By adopting this viewpoint, we have defined cities in relationship to a particular form of society—the state— and related different types of cities to various constellations of state power and urban economy. The predominant cultural role or function played by the city varies with its setting in state society, and this external adaptation conditions its internal organization and ideology. The five primary urban types—three representing cities before Western industrialism and two illustrating urban places after this industrial revolution— identify different forms of urban adaptation, organization, and ideology in relation to the nature of the wider (state) society.

The interests of the other urban anthropologies can be (and perhaps must be) integrated with this anthropology of urbanism for their mutual enhancement. For example, studies of the ghetto poor, the disfranchised alcoholic, and the excluded ethnic in America can say little about what is essentially urban in their behavior, or whether poverty, ethnicity, or alcoholism are universal urban characteristics. Such questions require a cross-cultural and typological view of cities such as this volume has attempted. Without this viewpoint, we might take what was found among the disfranchised of America as typical of all excluded populations, or what is even worse (for anthropologists), we might cease to care how the poor are organized in cities outside twentieth-century America.

The study of urbanization also profits from a broadened viewpoint. For instance, Oscar Lewis used his findings on Mexico City migrants to criticize an anthropological theory that identified urbanization with family breakdown, secularization, impersonality, and general social disorganization. Clearly, the urban villagers of colonial cities disprove such notions. In recognition of this fact, Lewis wrote that "urbanization is not a single, unitary, universally similar process but assumes different forms . . . depending upon the prevailing historic, economic, social and cultural conditions."[18] These forms are precisely what the urban typology proposed in this volume specifies. Studying the recent migrants to cities is therefore not sufficient to be able to specify the characteristics of urbanization; the cities to which the migrants come also determine how they adapt to their urban experience.

Other presumed universals of urban existence like rural-urban antagonism, heterogeneity, commerce, impersonality, or dense population have proved equally inapplicable to all cities when subjected to

---

[18]Lewis, "Urbanization Without Breakdown: A Case Study," *The Scientific Monthly*, LXXV, 1 (1952), p. 39.

cross-cultural scrutiny. Perhaps the ultimate conceit of Western or industrial nations and the social sciences they produced was to believe (at
least until recently) that all cities were like their own. We might allow
primitives their blowguns and lineages, peasants their plow oxen and
joint families, but that most complex of social institutions, the city, must
be made in our own image. Anthropologists have traditionally exploded
such ethnocentric ideas of Western superiority or uniqueness. We have
shown how different forms of marriage, kinship, and ideology arise and
prevail under certain cultural conditions, no matter how bizarre they
may appear to the outsider at first glance. It is time to take this orientation much further; we must take it into the cross-cultural study of cities
and urban institutions.

Bibliography

ABU-LUGHOD, JANET. "Migrant Adjustment to City Life: The Egyptian Case." *The American Journal of Sociology,* LXVII, 1 (1961).

ARENSBERG, CONRAD. "The Urban in Cross-Cultural Perspective," in *Urban Anthropology: Research Perspectives and Strategies,* Southern Anthropological Proceedings, Number 2, Elizabeth M. Eddy, ed. Athens: University of Georgia Press, 1968.

———— and SOLON T. KIMBALL, *Culture and Community.* New York: Harcourt, Brace & World, Inc., 1965.

BENET, FRANCISCO. "Sociology Uncertain: The Ideology of the Rural-Urban Continuum." *Comparative Studies in Society and History,* VI, 1 (1963).

BRUCKER, GENE A. *Renaissance Florence.* New York: John Wiley & Sons, Inc., 1969.

CHILDE, GORDON. *What Happened in History.* Baltimore, Maryland: Penguin Books, 1954.

COE, MICHAEL D. "Social Typology and the Tropical Forest Civilizations." *Comparative Studies in Society and History,* IV, 1 (1961), pp. 65–85.

———— "A Model of Lowland Maya Community Structure." *Southwestern Journal of Anthropology,* XXI, 2 (1965), pp. 97–114.

COHEN, ABNER. *Custom and Politics in Urban Africa: A Study of Hausa Migrants in Yoruba Towns.* Berkeley: University of California Press, 1969.

DAHL, ROBERT A. *Who Governs?: Democracy and Power in an American City.* New Haven: Yale University Press, 1964.

FOX, RICHARD G. "Resiliency and Change in the Indian Caste System: The Umar of U.P." *The Journal of Asian Studies,* XXVI, 4 (1967).

———— *From Zamindar to Ballot Box: Community Change in a North Indian Market Town.* Ithaca, New York: Cornell University Press, 1969.

————"Rajput 'Clans' and Rurban Settlements in Northern India," in *Urban India: Society, Space and Image,* Richard G. Fox, ed. Durham, North Carolina: Program in Comparative Studies on Southern Asia, Duke University, 1970.

———— *Kin, Clan, Raja and Rule: State-Hinterland Relations in Preindustrial India.* Berkeley: University of California Press, 1971.

———— "Rationale and Romance in Urban Anthropology." *Urban Anthropology,* I, 2 (1972).

FRIED, MORTON H. *The Evolution of Political Society: An Essay in Political Anthropology.* New York: Random House, 1967.

GANS, HERBERT J. *The Urban Villagers: Group and Class in the Life of Italian-Americans.* New York: Free Press, 1962.

GEERTZ, CLIFFORD. "The Development of the Javanese Economy: A Socio-Cultural Approach." Cambridge, Massachusetts: Center for International Studies, M.I.T., mimeo, 1956.

———— *The Social History of an Indonesian Town.* Cambridge, Massachusetts: The M.I.T. Press, 1965.

———— "Politics Past, Politics Present: Some Notes on the Uses of Anthropology in Understanding the New States." *Archives Européennes de Sociologie,* VIII, 1 (1967).

———— *Agricultural Involution: The Process of Ecological Change in Indonesia.* Berkeley: University of California Press, 1968.

GOTTMAN, JEAN. *Megalopolis The Urbanized Northeastern Seaboard of the United States.* Cambridge, Massachusetts: The M.I.T. Press, 1961.

GUERARD, ALBERT. *The Life and Death of an Ideal: France in the Classical Age.* New York: Charles Scribner's Sons, 1928.

GULICK, JOHN. *Tripoli: A Modern Arab City.* Cambridge, Massachusetts: Harvard University Press, 1967.

———— "Urban Anthropology: Its Present and Future," in *Readings in*

Anthropology, 2nd edition, Morton H. Fried, ed. New York: Thomas Y. Crowell Company, 1968.

GUTKIND, E.A. *International History of City Development*, Volume I: *Urban Development in Central Europe*. New York: The Free Press of Glencoe, 1964.

————— *International History of City Development*, Volume V: *Urban Development in Western Europe: France and Belguim*. New York: The Free Press of Glencoe, 1970.

HALL, JOHN WHITNEY. "The Castle Town and Japan's Modern Urbanization." *The Far Eastern Quarterly*, XV, 1 (1955).

HANNERZ, ULF. *Soulside: Inquiries into Ghetto Culture and Community*. New York: Columbia University Press, 1969.

————— "Ethnicity and Opportunity in Urban America," in *Urban Ethnicity*, Abner Cohen, ed. London: Tavistock Publications, 1974.

HEINE-GELDERN, ROBERT. "Conceptions of State and Kingship in Southeast Asia." *The Far Eastern Quarterly*, II, 1 (1942), pp. 15–30.

HIBBERT, A.B. "The Origins of the Medieval Town Patriciate." *Past and Present*, III (1953).

HOURANI, A.H. "Introduction: The Islamic City in the Light of Recent Research," in *Papers on Islamic History: I. The Islamic City: A Colloquium*, A.H. Hourani and S.M. Stern, eds. Oxford: Bruno Cassirer Ltd., 1970.

HYDE, J.K. *Padua in the Age of Dante*. Manchester, England: Manchester University Press, 1966.

KROEBER, A.L. and CLYDE KLUCKHOHN. *Culture: A Critical Review of Concepts and Definitions*. Cambridge, Massachusetts: The Museum, 1952.

KUPER, HILDA. *An African Aristocracy: Rank Among the Swazi*. London: Oxford University Press, 1947.

LAPIDUS, IRA MARVIN. *Muslim Cities in the Later Middle Ages*. Cambridge, Massachusetts: Harvard University Press, 1967.

————— "Muslim Cities and Islamic Societies," in *Middle Eastern Cities: A Symposium on Ancient, Islamic, and Contemporary Middle Eastern Urbanism*, Ira M. Lapidus, ed. Berkeley: University of California Press, 1969.

————— "Muslim Urban Society in Mamluk Syria," in *Papers on Islamic History: I. The Islamic City: A Colloquium*, A.H. Hourani and S.M. Stern, eds. Oxford: Bruno Cassirer Ltd., 1970.

LEEDS, ANTHONY. "The Anthropology of Cities: Some Methodological Issues," in *Urban Anthropology: Research Perspectives and Strategies* Southern Anthropological Proceedings, Number 2, Elizabeth M. Eddy, ed. Athens, University of Georgia Press, 1968.

———— "The Significant Variables Determining the Character of Squatter Settlements." *America Latina*, XII, 3 (1969).

LERNER, DANIEL. "Comparative Analysis of Processes of Modernisation," in *The City in Modern Africa*, Horace Miner, ed. London: Pall Mall Press, 1967.

LEWIS, OSCAR. "Urbanization Without Breakdown: A Case Study." *The Scientific Monthly*, LXXV, 1 (1952).

———— "Further Observations on the Folk-Urban Continuum and Urbanization with Special Reference to Mexico City," in *The Study of Urbanization*, Philip M. Hauser and Leo F. Schnore, eds. New York: John Wiley & Sons, Inc., 1965.

———— *La Vida: A Puerto Rican Family in the Culture of Poverty—San Juan and New York*. New York: Vintage Books, A Division of Random House, 1968.

LIEBOW, ELLIOT. *Tally's Corner: A Study of Negro Streetcorner Men*. Boston: Little, Brown and Company, 1967.

LITTLE, KENNETH LINDSAY. *West African Urbanization: A Study of Voluntary Associations in Social Change*. Cambridge: The University Press, 1965.

———— "Urbanization and Regional Associations: Their Paradoxical Function," in *Urban Anthropology: Cross-Cultural Studies of Urbanization*, Aidan Southall, ed. New York: Oxford University Press, 1973.

LOPEZ, ROBERT S. "The Trade of Medieval Europe: The South," in *The Cambridge Economic History of Europe*, Volume II: *Trade and Industry in the Middle Ages*, M.M. Postan, E.E. Rich, and Edward Miller, eds. Cambridge: The University Press, 1963.

MCKINNEY, JOHN C. "Sociological Theory and the Process of Typification," in *Theoretical Sociology: Perspectives and Development*, John C. McKinney and Edward A. Tiryakian, eds. Englewood Cliffs, New Jersey: Prentice-Hall, Inc., 1970.

MANGIN, WILLIAM. *Peasants in Cities: Readings in the Anthropology of Urbanization*, William Mangin, ed. Boston: Houghton Mifflin Company, 1970.

———— "Sociological, Cultural, and Political Characteristics of Some Urban Migrants in Peru," in *Urban Anthropology: Cross-Cultural Studies of Urbanization*, Aidan Southall, ed. New York: Oxford University Press, 1973.

MARRIOTT, McKIM. "Little Communities in an Indigenous Civilization," in *Village India: Studies in the Little Community*, McKim Marriott, ed. Chicago: University of Chicago Press, 1955.

MINER, HORACE. "The City and Modernisation: An Introduction," in *The City in Modern Africa*, Horace Miner, ed. London: Pall Mall Press, 1967.

MITCHELL, J. CLYDE, *The Kalela Dance: Aspects of Social Relationships Among Urban Africans in Northern Rhodesia*. Rhodes-Livingstone Institute, Paper No. 27. Manchester, England: University Press, 1956.

_____ "Theoretical Orientations in African Urban Studies," in *The Social Anthropology of Complex Societies*, Michael Banton, ed. London: Tavistock Publications, 1966.

_____ *Social Networks in Urban Situations: Analyses of Personal Relationships in Central African Towns*, J. Clyde Mitchell, ed. Manchester, England: Manchester University Press, 1969.

MOORE, KENNETH. "The City as Context: Context as Process." *Urban Anthropology*, IV, 1 (Spring, 1975).

MUNDY, JOHN HINE. *Liberty and Political Power in Toulouse, 1050–1230*. New York: Columbia University Press, 1954.

MUNZ, PETER. *Life in the Age of Charlemagne*. New York: Putnam, 1969.

MURPHEY, RHOADS. "The City as a Center of Change: Western Europe and China," in *Readings in Cultural Geography*, Philip Wagner and Marvin W. Mikesell, eds. Chicago: University of Chicago Press, 1962.

NEALE, WALTER C. *Economic Change in Rural India: Land Tenure and Reform in Uttar Pradesh, 1800–1955*. New Haven: Yale University Press, 1962.

PARK, ROBERT E., ERNEST W. BURGESS, and RODERICK D. McKENZIE. *The City*. Chicago: University of Chicago Press, 1925.

PIRENNE, HENRI. *Medieval Cities: Their Origins and the Revival of Trade*, trans. by Frank D. Halsey. Princeton: Princeton University Press, 1925.

RANUM, OREST. *Paris in the Age of Absolutism: An Essay*. New York: John Wiley & Sons, Inc., 1968.

REDFIELD, ROBERT. *The Folk Culture of Yucatan*. Chicago: University of Chicago Press, 1941.

_____ "The Folk Society." *The American Journal of Sociology*, LII, 4 (1947).

_____ and Milton Singer, "The Cultural Role of Cities." *Economic Development and Culture Change*, III, 1 (1954).

RIGGS, FRED W. *Administration in Developing Countries: The Theory of Prismatic Society*. Boston: Houghton Mifflin Company, 1964.

_____ *Thailand: The Modernization of a Bureaucratic Polity*. Honolulu: East-West Center Press, 1966.

ROLLWAGEN, JACK R. "Introduction." *Urban Anthropology*, IV, 1 (Spring, 1975).

_____ "The City as Context: The Puerto Ricans of Rochester, New York." *Urban Anthropology*, IV, 1 (Spring, 1975).

RÖRIG, FRITZ. *The Medieval Town*. Berkeley: University of California Press, 1967.

ROWE, WILLIAM L. "Caste, Kinship, and Association in Urban India," in *Urban Anthropology: Cross-Cultural Studies of Urbanization*, Aidan Southall, ed. New York: Oxford University Press, 1973.

SHACK, W.A. "Urban Ethnicity and the Cultural Process of Urbanization in Ethiopia," in *Urban Anthropology: Cross-Cultural Studies of Urbanization*, Aidan Southall, ed. New York: Oxford University Press, 1973.

SHELDON, CHARLES DAVID. *The Rise of the Merchant Class in Tokugawa Japan, 1600–1868: An Introductory Survey*. Published for the Association of Asian Studies by J.J. Augustin Incorporated, Locust Valley, New York: 1958.

SINGER, MILTON. "The Expansion of Society and Its Cultural Implications," in *City Invincible: A Symposium on Urbanization and Cultural Development in the Ancient Near East*, Carl H. Kraeling and Robert M. Adams, eds. Chicago: University of Chicago Press, 1960.

SJOBERG, GIDEON. "The Preindustrial City." *The American Journal of Sociology*, LX, 5 (1955).

_____ *The Preindustrial City, Past and Present*. New York: The Free Press, 1960.

SKINNER, G. WILLIAM. "Chinese Peasants and the Closed Community: An Open and Shut Case." *Comparative Studies in Society and History*, XIII (1971).

SMITH, M. ESTELLIE. "A Tale of Two Cities: The Reality of Historical Differences." *Urban Anthropology*, IV, 1 (Spring, 1975).

SPRADLEY, JAMES P. *You Owe Yourself a Drunk: An Ethnography of Urban Nomads.* Boston: Little, Brown and Company, 1970.

SOUTHALL, AIDAN W. *Alur Society: A Study in Processes and Types of Domination.* Cambridge: W. Heffer & Sons Limited, n.d.

THRUPP, SYLVIA. "The Creativity of Cities: A Review Article." *Comparative Studies in Society and History,* IV, 1 (1961).

VALENTINE, CHARLES A. *Culture and Poverty: Critique and Counter-Proposals.* Chicago: University of Chicago Press, 1968.

VAN WERVEKE, H. "The Rise of the Towns," in *The Cambridge Economic History of Europe,* Volume III: *Economic Organization and Politics in the Middle Ages,* M.M. Postan, E.E. Rich, and Edward Miller, eds. Cambridge: The University Press, 1963.

VON GRUNEBAUM, G.E., *Islam: Essays in the Nature and Growth of a Cultural Tradition.* Memoirs of the American Anthropological Association, Memoir #81, *The American Anthropologist,* LVII, 2, Part 2 (1955).

WADDELL, JACK O. and O. MICHAEL WATSON. *The American Indian in Urban Society.* Boston: Little, Brown and Company, 1971.

WALSH, RICHARD. *Charleston's Sons of Liberty: A Study of the Artisans, 1763–1789.* Columbia: University of South Carolina Press, 1959.

WEBER, MAX. *The City,* trans. and ed. by Don Martindale and Gertrud Neuwirth. Glencoe, Illinois: The Free Press, 1958.

WHEATLEY, PAUL. *Pivot of the Four Quarters: A Preliminary Enquiry into the Origins and Character of the Ancient Chinese City.* Chicago: Aldine, 1971.

———— "The Concept of Urbanism," in *Man, Settlement, and Urbanism,* Peter J. Ucko, Ruth Tringham, and G.W. Dimbleby, eds. Cambridge: Schenkman, 1972.

WIRTH, LOUIS. "Urbanism as a Way of Life." *The American Journal of Sociology, XLIV,* 1 (1938).

WOLF, ERIC R. *Peasants.* Englewood Cliffs, New Jersey: Prentice-Hall, Inc. 1966.

YAZAKI, TAKEO. *Social Change and the City in Japan: From Earliest Times Through the Industrial Revolution,* trans. by David L. Swain. Japan Publications, Inc., 1968.

ZNANIECKI, FLORIAN and WILLIAM ISAAC THOMAS. *The Polish Peasant in Europe and America.* New York: Alfred A. Knopf, 1927.

Index

A

Acculturation, 13, 128–130
Adaptation, urban, 19–22, 45–46, 69–72, 110–111, 126–127, 150, 161
Adaptive strategies, 13–14, 127, 128–131, 144–147, 158
Anthropology:
  development of, 2–9, 58
  methods and viewpoints:
    cross-cultural comparison, 4, 9, 12, 15, 141, 161
    diachronic viewpoint, 7, 11, 14, 17, 20, 22, 24
    holism, 3, 4, 6–7, 9, 10, 22, 149, 157, 161
    participant-observation, 5–6, 7, 8
    pursuit of the exotic, 7–8, 12, 13
    synchronic viewpoint, 7, 144
Anthropology of poverty, 9, 12–14, 15, 16, 37, 38, 143, 149, 157, 159, 160
Anthropology of urbanism, 9–12, 16, 17, 24, 36, 38, 149, 157, 159–161
Anthropology of urbanization, 14–16, 37, 160
Arensberg, Conrad, 10, 55
Ascriptive roles, 42, 64, 85, 121

B

Brokers, 86, 129, 158–159 (*see also* Urban notables)
Bureaucratic state, 34, 62–65, 67, 69, 71, 84, 87, 95, 111
Burgess, Robert, 59

C

Childe, V. Gordon, 23
Cities:
  and societies, 18–24
  and states, 24–29, 32–34
  cultural roles, 10–11, 18, 32–34, 35 (*see also* Cultural roles)
    administrative, 32–33, 60–61
    colonial, 118, 139
    heterogenetic, 11